SKYLINE LONDON

Caroline Dale attended Camden School for Girls in North London and read Chinese at the University of Leeds. She has worked as a writer, journalist, foreign correspondent and stockbroker of equities and derivatives in London and Tokyo. Today, as a Blue Badge Guide, she specialises in walking tours of London, in English and Japanese, for her own company, reaLondon, www.reaLondon.net.

CAROLINE DALE

SKYLINE
LONDON

A GUIDE TO THE FINEST VIEWS FROM
THE CAPITAL'S HIGH POINTS

Aurum

First published in Great Britain 2012 by Aurum Press Ltd
7 Greenland Street, London NW1 0ND

www.aurumpress.co.uk

PHOTO CREDITS

© Herbert Müller: i, ii–iii, 15, 16, 17, 18, 23, 24, 26-7, 30, 31, 37, 40, 46, 47, 49,
57, 58, 59, 64, 65, 70, 71, 77, 78, 80, 81, 83, 85, 86, 87, 88-9, 92, 93, 98, 99, 106-
7, 109, 110-11, 113, 114, 115, 122, 123, 146, 147, 149, 150, 157, 158-9; Alamy:
20, 21, 34, 42-3, 44 (top), 54, 72-3, 74-5, 102-3, 106 (bottom), 119, 120, 130,
131, 132, 137, 138, 140, 141, 143, 144, 167; Mirrorpix: 151, 153, 154-5; Getty
Images: 95, 96, 128, 129, 164; Mary Evans: 161; Caroline Dale: 34, 166; Graham
Coster: 61, 62, 117; SushiSamba: 27 (top), 28; City Hall: 44 (bottom); Attic at
Pen Peninsula: 55; Altitude at Millbank Tower: 104; Rob Telford, Cybertects.
co.uk: ix, 10; Paul Wright: 14; ThisParticularGreg: 33; Rob Fuller, EZTD Images:
34; Abi Saffrey: 50; Debbie Timmins: 54; Leila Johnston: 67; Ewan Munro: 68;
Andrew Grill: 115; Jen and Stuart Robertson: 125; David Edwards, www.flickr.
com/photos/dhedwards: 126; Maxwell Hamilton: 131; Kaustav Bhattacharya
2012, www.flickr.com/photos/astrolondon: 134-5; Harshil Shah: 140; Simon
Kendrick: 163; Jo Neville, JoNeville.com: 166; Simon Crubellier: 168

Every effort has been made to trace the copyright holders of material quoted
in this book. If application is made in writing to the publisher, any omissions
will be included in future editions.

A catalogue record for this book is available from the British Library.

ISBN 978 1 84513 762 5

1 3 5 7 9 10 8 6 4 2

2012 2014 2016 2015 2013

Design by Carrdesignstudio.com
360°-view maps by Reginald Piggott
Height graph on pp. 4-5 and inside-front-cover map by Tim Peters

Printed in China

p.1 photograph: St Paul's seen in view west from Lloyd's of London.
pp. 2-3 photograph: The City, and Essex beyond, seen from the Shard.

CONTENTS

Introduction   vi

OPEN TO THE PUBLIC   9

Paramount at Centre Point   10

St Paul's Cathedral: Stone Gallery   15

One New Change   19

One, Poultry   22

SushiSamba at the Heron Tower   25

Vertigo at Tower 42   29

The Gherkin or 30 St Mary Axe   32

The Monument   36

City Hall   41

Tower Bridge Exhibition Walkway   45

Plateau at Canada Place   48

Attic Pan Peninsula   51

Holden Point   56

The Royal Victoria Dock Bridge   60

Trinity Buoy Wharf Lighthouse   63

Beckton Alp   66

Shooters Hill and Ankerdine
Crescent   69

Greenwich Park   72

Cerise Road Car Park, Peckham
Rye   76

The Point at Point Hill   79

Telegraph Hill Park   82

The Shard   84

Oxo Tower Building   88

Tate Modern   91

The Skylon at the Royal
Festival Hall   94

London Eye   97

Altitude 360 at Millbank Tower   102

Henman Hill   105

Westminster Cathedral Bell Tower   108

London Hilton on Park Lane   112

Waterstones 5th View   115

The National Portrait Gallery
Restaurant   118

The Sheraton Park Tower   121

Top Floor at Peter Jones   124

Babylon at Derry and Toms'   127

Richmond Hill   130

Horsenden Hill   133

Alexandra Palace   136

Parliament Hill   139

Primrose Hill   142

The New London Architecture
Model   145

Heights at St George's Hotel   148

CLOSED TO THE PUBLIC   151

One Canada Square   152

Lloyd's of London   156

Selfridges Roof Garden   160

The BT Tower   162

Trellick Tower   165

INTRODUCTION

If you lose your bearings in a big city, one of the best ways to re-orient yourself is to head for the top of a tall, central landmark. In Paris this would be the Eiffel Tower, from which you can fix on the east-west flow of the Seine. In New York, the Empire State Building provides a compass-style view of Manhattan framed by the East and Hudson Rivers.

Until now, London has had no similarly iconic building from which its citizens can find their sense of place or define their skyline. Indeed, London has resolutely avoided becoming a high-rise city at all. Moreover, its special topography resists such immediate formulations as New York or Paris with their grid-patterned streets. Neither does the Thames oblige with its sudden zigzag

curves – for example, where the City and Westminster meet, the river dislocates rather than instructs our bearings.

But in 2012 London will finally have its own iconic look-out structure: the Shard at London Bridge – a stunning splinter of glass on the city's skyline that, by a few metres, will become the tallest building in Europe. And in Spring 2013 its public observation gallery opens, with vertiginous views to vie with those from the London Eye. The Shard – followed by a forest of fellow skyscrapers like the Walkie-Talkie and the Cheesegrater already

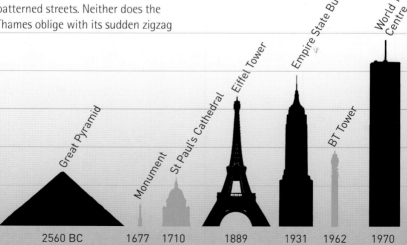

shooting up in its wake – is probably confirmation that London is now officially high-rise.

This new guidebook, published to commemorate the completion of the Shard, reminds us that London is a city wonderfully capable of revealing its best views. It is blessed with hills like Primrose, Telegraph and Horsenden that provide natural skyline viewpoints. Historic views of key cityscapes, like that of the rural Thames from Richmond Hill, have been protected from change (again, unlike Paris or New York) for centuries, and there is also a remarkable number of bars and restaurants at the top of London's tall buildings – many a well-kept secret – where you can dine or drink in front of dazzling vistas of the capital. Even a multistorey car park in Peckham and the slag heap of an old gasworks in east London offer unique revelations of London spread out below, while Henman Hill in Wimbledon is just as exciting for skyline spectators as for tennis.

Researching this book showed me how many of London's new tall buildings, turning up time and again in slightly different configurations, become strangely more animate than inanimate to the viewer. They have their good and bad days, not always presenting their most flattering

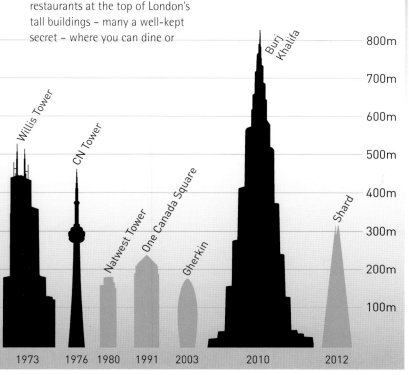

side. It's like spotting old friends in a crowd. The same cluster of buildings can look streamlined and perky in early morning sunlight, but a bit rough around the edges in a hazy evening hue.

You'll also see how, viewed from reciprocal locations, buildings inevitably develop relationships with each other – try the Paramount at Centre Point from the Hilton at Hyde Park, and then the other way around. What's more, some London skyline views are heartachingly fabulous at first sight, but then the magic fades. Others, subtler in character, mesmerise or play visual tricks. And you may find, as I did, that even the most banal swathe of Victorian rooftops, illuminated by the raking evening sunlight, can quicken the

pulse. All the 50-odd places covered in this book reveal in different ways how a disparate set of 'villages' coalesces into the one densely packed, visually rich, urban complex we call London.

CAROLINE DALE

Some of the places in this guide – hills and bridges – are accessible all the time; some are only open at certain times and charge an admission fee; for others you will have to book ahead and be prepared to buy a drink or have dinner. Some places are not open at all now to the public, but are included because they once were, and have their place in the history of London's skyline.

Please check opening information carefully before you visit any of them.

ACKNOWLEDGEMENTS

I would like to thank Aurum Press and my editors Graham Coster and Steve Gove for their whole-hearted support and innumerable, valuable contributions to this book. Also, I am enduringly grateful for photographer Herbert Müller's set of superb photographs that eloquently convey so much more than I could ever put into words.

I want to express my gratitude to the following people who generously found time and patience to assist me in gaining precious physical, as well as mental, access to many of these London skyline views. All being equally important, they are listed here in alphabetical order: Ashleigh Brayshaw, Mac Castro, Alexandra Coleman, Stephanie Ellers, Alan Forsyth, Darren Gearing, Tom Goodall, Aaron Hardy, John Hare, Jean Jeffrey, Paula King, Irina Kouletsis, Madlen Langmeyer, Imelda McAloon, Marie–Soleil Marsolais, Dan Pattinson, David Scripps, Carole Sim, Beth Stockley and Debbie Whitfield.

Opposite: *Renzo Piano's colourful Central St Giles development dominates the near ground in the view east from Paramount at Centre Point, with New Oxford Street stretching away towards Holborn*

OPEN TO THE PUBLIC

PARAMOUNT AT CENTRE POINT

A VIEW FROM THE VERY CENTRE OF LONDON, EQUIDISTANT FROM ST PAUL'S TO THE EAST AND MARBLE ARCH TO THE WEST

Designed in Brutalist style by the late Richard Seifert in 1966 for property mogul Harry Hyams, Centre Point attracted controversy from the outset, as nothing like it in height (380ft) or appearance had been seen in London's West End before. Architectural historian Nikolaus Pevsner described it as 'coarse in the extreme'. Anger followed Hyams' refusal to fill the building unless he could find a single company to occupy it; in the 1970s it was targeted by squatters, increasing its notoriety. As architectural aesthetics developed, Centre Point achieved Grade II listed status in 1995. In 2008 a members' club known as the Paramount Club opened on the top three floors.

Address 101-103 New Oxford Street, WC1A 1DD
Nearest Tube Tottenham Court Road
Open To The Public? Member's club – admission only by ringing ahead to add name to guest list
Disabled accessibility Yes
Website www.paramount.uk.net
Contact details 020 7420 2900

With Tottenham Court Road station a major hub of the Crossrail project, a new ticket hall and platforms are currently under construction at the crossroads of Oxford Street and Charing Cross Road, literally at the foot of Centre Point. Meanwhile, the top floor of the Paramount Club provides an indoor viewing gallery around Centre Point's four sides. The view is unusually good thanks to the building's location at the very centre point of London, equidistant between St Paul's to the east and Marble Arch to the west.

WEST

It is said that as London moves ever eastwards, the proliferation of high-rise buildings in that direction has left an imbalance of dramatic skyline views to the west. Not so from the Paramount, where the view westwards is a treat. In the far distance a rare view of the full span of Harrow on the Hill is appreciated – all the more so now the iconic arch of Wembley Stadium, 1033ft from end to end, sets the stage in front. As the planes descend towards Heathrow, London's westward vista becomes undeniably more patrician with its huge expanses of parks and squares including St James's Park, Hyde Park,

The Wembley Arch in the far distance, with Oxford Street stretching west all the way to Hyde Park.

Green Park, Grosvenor and Hanover Squares all clearly visible.

In contrast, the low-rise conservation area of Soho sits immediately below. Soho's boundaries are easy to trace as it expands from tree-filled squares in a geometric grid that is not easy to appreciate walking its narrow, dense and congested streets. From up here its gentle heights belie its character as a largely office and retail rather than residential sector.

Further west, Oxford Street's first diagonal crossing at Oxford Circus catches the eye as an orientation point. Close beside it is the pale stone superstructure of the London College of Fashion, recessed above its ground floor row of shops. There is a fine view of its neighbour John Lewis, built in similar stone with Barbara Hepworth's aluminium sculpture *Winged Figure* (1962) on the wall facing us.

NORTH

St Pancras' Renaissance Hotel with its Gothic-inspired towers and turrets grabs the sightline, setting off the broad flat white roof of Arsenal Football Club's Emirates Stadium in Islington that rises like a flying saucer about to take flight from the hill behind.

In the foreground, Bedford Square, built in 1775 and today the most intact of London's squares, shows off a rare sight of its secret backside. The terrace of houses on its southern flank appears from above like a lateral, evenly spaced wave of alternate bow and flat grey brick elevations punctuated in their height by elegant bay windows – a contrast to the classical flat Georgian fronts seen from the street side. And what generous long gardens for a central London location!

There is also a much better understanding at this level of the new extension – the World Conservation and Exhibitions Centre – designed by Rogers Stirk Harbour at the north side of the British Museum. A jumble of outbuildings and temporary structures are being cleared away for

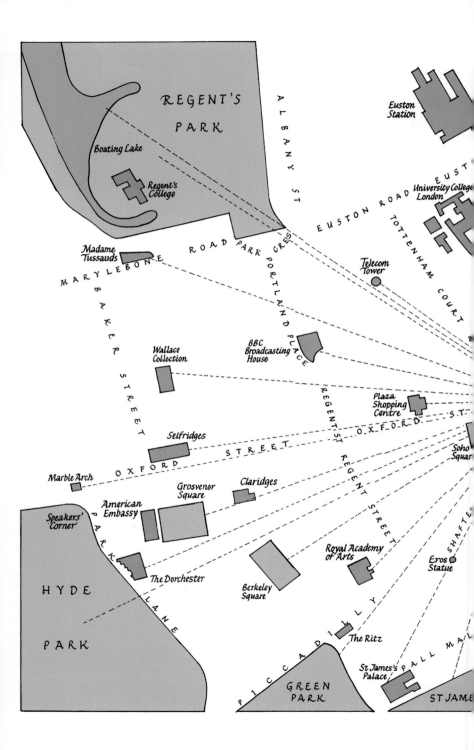

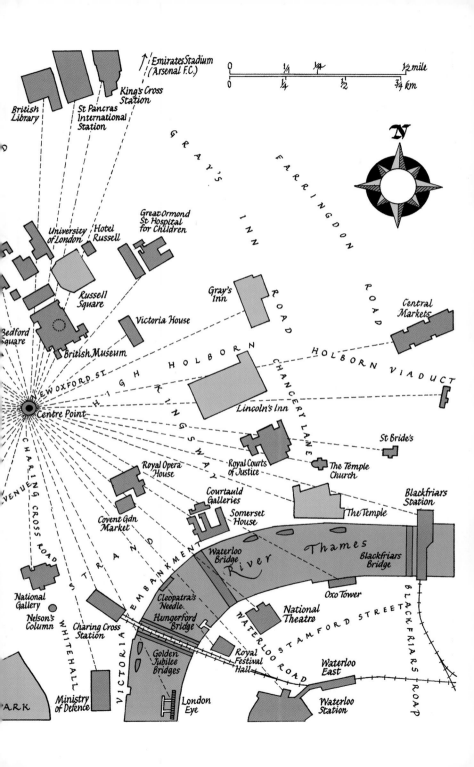

four linked pavilions that will provide almost 11,000 square feet of new exhibition space plus accommodation for conservators.

Other surprises likely to elude the eye at ground level include the twin bright green tiled turrets above the Hotel Russell's main entrance on Russell Square, their colour contrasting wildly with its terracotta-clad façade. The zigzag concrete 'W' shape of the YMCA is visible on the corner of Tottenham Court Road and Great Russell Street, and a slice of the Brunswick Estate's gleaming white stepped terrace frontage protrudes into the street close to Coram's Fields behind. The white stone façade of Victoria House that runs the entire length of Bloomsbury Square's east flank has 14 massive ionic pillars that look far more imposing from 400 feet up than at street level.

EAST

Looking from the east window, directly below New Oxford Street snakes east in a straight line as it segues seamlessly into Holborn, appearing to stop abruptly as it reaches the grey concrete of the Barbican complex beyond. To the south of the Barbican, the gathering of giant cranes constructing Crossrail's Farringdon Station appear just a nod away from those about to finish construction of the brand new station complex at Blackfriars. The station is the first in London to be built on the railway bridge itself and served by entrances on both sides of the Thames.

Slightly nearer, to the south-east the hulking grey Masonic Temple (London's favourite movie location inside and out) broods beside a white unbroken bulk – at first unrecognisable from this height. This can only be the rooftop fly-tower that houses working platforms and scenery storage above the stage of the Royal Opera House, Covent Garden from an angle previously unseen, and looking even stranger as Waterloo Bridge appears to tail southwards out of its rear.

The fabulous nightscape to the southeast of Centre Point, from the City round to the Shard.

ST PAUL'S CATHEDRAL: STONE GALLERY

LONDON REVEALED FROM ST PAUL'S

Sir Christopher Wren was appointed to rebuild St Paul's Cathedral, the cathedral of the Diocese of London, following the Great Fire of 1666 that destroyed old St Paul's. It was begun in 1675 and more or less completed by 1710 – an astounding feat by one man in his lifetime for those days. The reconstruction of London was paid for by an Act of Parliament that raised the tax on coal arriving in London to three shillings per ton. Fourpence halfpenny of that sum was allocated towards rebuilding St Paul's.

Address St Paul's Churchyard, top of Ludgate Hill, EC4M 8AD
Nearest Tube St Paul's
Open To The Public? Opening hours; Mon-Sat, 9:30am-4:15pm, entrance charge
Disabled accessibility No
Website www.stpauls.co.uk
Contact details 020 7246 8350

The golden cross on top of St Paul's Cathedral stands 365ft above the pavement. Once inside, continue climbing from the Whispering Gallery 100ft above the floor of the church, from where the paintings made by James Thornhill on the inner dome can best be viewed, and you arrive at the Stone Gallery, 170ft above ground level. This is the first outside viewpoint of London from St Paul's. The gallery is at the base of the outer dome, on top of its colonnade. Although it is 152 steps below the highest outside gallery (the Golden Gallery on top of the outer dome, just under the lantern) the view through the stone balustrade at this level seems more poignant, revealing and rooted in the atmosphere of Wren's London. From the confines of the Golden Gallery the view becomes too narrow and restricted.

SOUTH

The design of the Millennium Bridge immediately below looks its best

The Millennium Bridge leading to Tate Modern.

The unfinished Shard already dwarfs Guy's Hospital tower, with a train sweeping round to cross Cannon Street railway bridge.

from the Stone Gallery. The crowds crossing the bridge become part of its colour and dynamic shape. Far from seeming smaller at this height, the bridge's presence and importance is magnified.

Beyond, to the south, the railway bridge of Cannon Street Station emerges from between the twin Victorian brick water towers – relics of the age of steam. On the south bank the tracks snake around the backs of the few remaining 19th-century riverbank wharves in a sweeping high-level curve at London Bridge, embracing the magnificent elongated latter-day pyramid of Renzo Piano's unfinished Shard, the

UK's tallest construction. Back on this side of the river, the wonders of the new Cannon Street Station's modern engineering, based on suspension bridge techniques, are visible in three sets of giant steel cross-frames.

NORTH

On the opposite side of the gallery, the three rust-red terracotta, beige granite and green glazed pavilions of Bishopsgate Exchange, flanking the Bishopsgate side of Liverpool Street Station, also take on a new substance and presence. Walking through their linking arcade just above street level, their sheer bulk is never perceived.

From up here it rings absolutely true that at the end of the 1980s, during the City's post-Big Bang rebuild, this was the largest building site in Europe. Twenty-five years on, the 500-acre site of the Olympic Park in turn became Europe's largest building site; the white Olympic Stadium's ellipsoidal roof, with the tangled red tubes of Anish Kapoor's 377ft sculpture Orbit beside it, rises as if directly beyond the Exchange's green atria roofs.

EAST

Looking due east, the new Walbrook complex with its low sloping domed roof and façade, wrapped by black horizontal carbon-fibre louvres, looks as if it is about to hound out the delicate golden finials of St Mary Aldermary's stone tower a stone's throw away. On a cloudy day any colour in the City close by stands out, like the slice of red glass roof over Jean Nouvel's One New Change and the bright green slab of grass of the restored garden of St Augustine's Church, bombed in the Second World War.

Further to the east the iconic towers of the City skyline sit directly in front of their younger peers at Canary Wharf. That prominent little 'nuclear family' cluster of 1930s art nouveau radio-inspired glass roofs on the corner of Gracechurch and Lombard Streets was formerly the headquarters of Barclays Bank. The curves contrast with the sharp-edged

East from St Paul's, with the One New Change 'stealth bomber' in the foreground, and the black Walbrook complex middle right behind St Mary Aldermary's.

upper steps of Norman Foster's new black glass Willis Building next door.

WEST

From the other side of the Gallery, the Cathedral's two west towers are seen to be ornamented on top with two perfect golden pineapples. So large and bright where we stand, they are barely noticeable from ground level. Perhaps this view of the Cathedral yields more than Wren intended. Looking immediately downwards there are grey slate roofs, lower in height, either side of the nave roof, and it becomes evident that there are two layers of walls on either side of the nave. The outer wall is higher than the upper storey wall of the nave itself. From up here this extra height is revealed to be a curtain wall, a device to conceal vital buttresses that support the clerestory of the nave.

It is slightly shocking to discover from up here that Wren's favourite sculptor, Francis Bird, did not execute the statue of St Paul that stands on the apex of the pediment of the west entrance (or those of the other apostles either side of him) in the round. From the Stone Gallery Paul, James and Peter with his cockerel at his feet all have flat backs!

The other revelation has little to do with the skyline but more to do with Wren's architecture itself. As you leave the Stone Gallery to ascend the steps to the Golden Gallery, the inner brick-built cone that secretly supports the stone and gold lantern on top of the outer wooden, lead-covered dome becomes visible all the way up.

Ludgate Hill looking west framed by St Paul's two pineapple-topped west towers.

ONE NEW CHANGE

FRESH VIEWS OF ST PAUL'S

When newly built mixed-use office, shopping and eating plaza One New Change opened in the City in October 2010, it signalled the Square Mile's whole-hearted intention to become a new seven-day destination for dining and upmarket retail therapy as well as for international business and finance. Nicknamed the 'stealth bomber' by its architect, Jean Nouvel, One New Change has proved everyone can spend more time (and money) in the City now that the South Bank's Tate Modern and Globe Theatre have been linked to St Paul's and the City via the Millennium Bridge. Thousands of visitors cross the bridge to combine a visit to St Paul's with an exploration of the cut and thrust of weekday Square Mile life. In its design two lost passageways from the medieval City grid have been reinstated, enabling fresh appreciation at ground level of the Cathedral's magnificent scale and structure. But not just at ground level. Nouvel has built the general public access to a skyline panorama from a height that has never been accessible before.

Address Cheapside, EC4M 9AF
Nearest Tube St Paul's
Open To The Public? 10am till late, 7days a week
Disabled accessibility Yes
Website www.onenewchange.com
Contact details 020 7002 8900

Let the shoppers and foodies enjoy the basement, ground and second floors but for lasting thrills stay in the glass lift sited in the core of the development and travel up to the top floor, Floor 6, to relish the body and dome of St Paul's Cathedral. Outside, visitors can enjoy a quiet haven above the crowds. As the brown glass roof slopes away in wings on either side it is clear why Nouvel dubbed his design 'the stealth bomber', a description meaningless from the ground. Make your way to the edge to appreciate the greatest architect of London's finest contribution to its skyline.

After Old St Paul's literally blew up and melted into the streets in the great 1666 conflagration, Sir Christopher Wren was commissioned by the City fathers, clergy and royalty to rebuild over 40 churches including London's most important, the seat of the Bishops of London, St Paul's Cathedral. Wren had set his heart on a new domed cathedral displaying all the best of classical Greek and Roman architectural concepts. The clergy were equally intent on achieving a Gothic design. The 'Warrant Design' was Wren's last desperate plan to win agreement from the clergy,

The first chance in centuries to consider the ingenious engineering by which Sir Christopher Wren supported the huge stone lantern atop St Paul's dome.

but the building today bears little resemblance to it.

From the top of Jean Nouvel's building some of Wren's contrivances, hidden for years, appear for the first time for all to marvel at. Looking straight ahead, it is clear at such close quarters that the outer dome, made of wood covered in lead, could never support the huge stone lantern we see sitting on top. Hidden inside the outer dome Wren built a brick cone to take the weight of the lantern. The cone rests on the inside recesses of the podium, the columns making that skyline signature dome merely a perfect shape without function. At this height and proximity we can see across the inner dome the windows of the other side with the light coming through. But the layer of windows above these real ones are revealed to be blind decorative fakes.

WEST

Beyond St Paul's in this direction, the clock tower of the Houses of Parliament stands directly behind the spokes of the London Eye. Next to it can be seen the full span of One Whitehall Court's very romantic French-looking roofs. On the other side of the Eye stands King's Reach Tower on the banks of the Thames by Blackfriars Bridge, and beside it the Sea Containers apartment block. Through a corridor of structures in the distance, the four white chimneys of Battersea's power station form another notable landmark.

SOUTHEAST

There is no view due east from here, but to the southeast the famous skyline landmarks of the 21st-century City of London like Tower 42, the stepped Heron Tower, Norman Foster's Gherkin (more correctly, 30 St Mary Axe) and the unfinished Shard catch the eye. We also get an unusual view of the two water towers that frame the tunnelled exit of Cannon Street Station on the Thames' side.

SOUTH

Turning southwards, looking beyond the blue glass Blue Fin building and the charcoal-grey and bright red

girders of the three tall Neo Bankside towers beside Tate Modern, we can see one possible reason why the wind turbines on the roof of the Strata, the new stripy black and white residential tower at Elephant and Castle, do not turn. Designed to reduce the residents' fuel bills – this is the first building in the world to have turbines integrated into its structure – they face 45 degrees in the wrong direction to catch London's prevailing westerly wind.

Due south on a clear day even the Crystal Palace transmission tower on Sydenham Hill is easy to spot. But the scene-stealer of the view from One New Change is unmistakably Wren's St Paul's.

The Shard and Guy's Tower in the view southeast from One New Change.

NUMBER ONE, POULTRY

HIDDEN GEMS OF THE CITY OF LONDON

Throughout its lengthy planning stages, One, Poultry managed to ruffle so many feathers that it is amazing it was ever built. Unveiled in 1997, its colourful façade – pinky-beige matt Australian sandstone with a patina like annual rings of wood combined with a pink-and-black-flecked shiny Gloucestershire stone – caused a big stir. Nicknamed the Titanic for its ship's prow-shaped corner and the Streaky Bacon or Rhubarb and Custard for its colour, for City workers the attraction was the Square Mile's first al fresco roof restaurant, Coq d'Argent. The name references the building's address on the site of a medieval live bird market and is a tribute to its architect, the late James Stirling.

Address EC2R 8EJ

Nearest Tube Bank

Open To The Public? Must book a table online or via the contact number

Disabled accessibility Yes

Website www.coqdargent.co.uk

Contact details 020 7395 5000

On the top of One, Poultry is a triangular roof garden with a real lawn, the grass framed by low chevrons of privet. At the apex of the V, from a curved 'safety' window, a secluded open turret with a low curved granite seat inside gives an arc-shaped view eastwards of Bank Junction. The arc sweeps round to include a backdrop of City icons: from north to south the Stock Exchange with Tower 42 just behind, Lloyds of London, the top two steps of the Willis Building, the top two glass-framed barrel roofs of Barclays, a single steep gable of Minster Court poking out by Ove Arup's Plantation Place and the

core of Raphael Vinoly's new 20 Fenchurch Street, aka the Walkie Talkie. The roof of Number One Poultry feels low enough for an intimate connection with its immediate surroundings but high enough to discover some hidden gems, because none of these old City buildings – mostly banks and insurance company headquarters – were built to be looked at from this height.

EAST

A beautiful gold grasshopper weathervane on top of the Royal Exchange's glass atrium roof was the family emblem of mid-16th-century financier and Lord Mayor Thomas Gresham, who built the first Exchange on this site in 1565. From up here it is revealed that the row of top windows in the forbidding curtain wall of John Soane's Bank of England is clearly made up of 18th-century blanks. Across the road on Cornhill, the City headquarters of Lloyds Bank changed hands in 2003. The listed building was stripped out except for its fine old ground-floor banking hall to accommodate smaller offices and retail space. But unseen from ground level are five additional storeys to the roofline, massive and stepped back, as well as an entirely new side extension complete with external glass-covered staircases.

On the roof garden, two stubby nautical wing balconies flare out on the north and south of Number One Poultry's east-facing turret beak. Standing on the decking surface of either wing there is a vertiginous view straight down through the gap that separates the balconies from the

granite-topped, razor sharp edges of beige stone jutting out from the building proper. From these glass-balustraded balconies, the edges of the building on the other side of the drop look like diving boards because there is no barrier. Looking straight down to street level at Cheapside through the glass is for strong stomachs only. Better to look straight ahead.

NORTH

From the north balcony, the top floors of the old Midland Bank headquarters in pale beige stone can be seen in the foreground, with a low lead-panelled dome never seen from street level. The skyline consists of one white Portland stone building after another as far as Moorgate, where the 'D'-shaped glass façade of Moor House meets City Point's vertical glass cylinder with its overhanging roof.

SOUTH

From the south balcony, the immense empty land mass left by the demolition of Temple Court and Bucklersbury House can be seen. A new complex called Bloomberg Square is planned to rise from here, dwarfing the 19th-century buildings that survive on the south side of Cannon Street. Until late 2013 there is an opportunity to enjoy for the last time – or at least for 25 years

The Gherkin towers over the Royal Exchange to the east of One, Poultry.

Left to right: the louvred exterior of the Walbrook building; the Rothschild headquarters; St Stephen Walbrook – to the south of One, Poultry.

– views across this quarter of the City. A cameo of four historic City institution roofs clusters between the site and Bank Junction. Rising high above the southern end of the 18th-century Mansion House, traditionally home to the Lord Mayors of the City, are the three non-matching glass elements of Rothschild's new headquarters – the oldest city bank to be founded and remain on this site. Next to these is the green dome of Wren's 17th-century St Stephen Walbrook, with its grey stone bell tower beside it. Providing a background contrast is the north and east façade of the new Walbrook building, shaded from the sun by its black louvred exterior.

SOUTHWEST

From the southwest-facing terrace on the restaurant's roof it is clear how Tate Modern on the invisible Thames at Bankside has been the catalyst for an almighty surge in new building. Despite the tangle of railway lines just a quarter of a mile to the south, the layers of new builds in all sizes continue. The business buildings, like the Blue Fin next to the bright brown brick façades of its neighbouring Bankside 123 complex and the grey and red girders of Neo Bankside by Tate Modern, are the eye-catchers of Southwark Street. From here a 'forest' of new and retrofitted blocks edge all the way south to the Strata in its stripy pyjamas at Elephant and Castle.

SUSHISAMBA AT THE HERON TOWER

THE HIGHEST OUTDOOR VIEWS IN LONDON, OVER THE CITY AND EAST END

Up close to the Gherkin and now dwarfed by the Shard's height, the Heron Tower registered its elegant impact on London's City skyline on completion in 2011. The new architectural must-have, external bracing down the north façade, identifies the building and its interior division into separate three-floor units arranged around internal atriums. The Heron's south-side windows are fitted in chocolate-bar squares of blue photovoltaic cells that double as sun shading. They partially obscure the transparent lifts travelling at 15 miles per hour from ground to roof. On the top floor of the Heron, SushiSamba offers three floors of dining. Better still, its two open terraces have for the first time given Londoners the option to experience outdoor eating, drinking and socialising 577ft above ground level.

Address 110 Bishopsgate, EC2N 4AY

Nearest Tube Liverpool Street

Open To The Public? Only for dining at SushiSamba restaurant by prior booking

Disabled accessibility Yes

Website www.sushisamba.com

Contact details 07946 876 880

The restaurant's two dedicated glass lifts are accessed outside at street level on Bishopsgate. Racing up to the 38th floor, time does not even allow your ears to pop before you step into the top 'village' – as each three-floor unit inside the Heron is known. SushiSamba occupies the tower's highest inhabited three floors in a separate 'standalone' unit. Its unique top terraces, paved in York stone, open London out by almost 360 degrees. The remaining southern and western vistas, featuring respectively the Shard and Strata, St Paul's and the BT Tower, are all visible from the windows inside.

NORTH

Out on the larger rectangular North Terrace, the glass of the building's atrium roof sits just beyond the terrace itself distancing the view due north. We are so high up that the view goes straight to the edge of the City of London and a new skyline feature half a mile away – the recently reopened London Overground East London Line. This great swathe of grey concrete running east–west encases the high-level tracks and new Shoreditch High Street Station. A small patch of unregenerated empty green scrubland left over from the Blitz is still identifiable below – a precious reminder of a bitter past.

To the left of the station is the new double-arch white railway bridge going over the main road at the point where Bishopsgate becomes Shoreditch High Street. And to the left of that, a little closer to the Heron, are the upper floors of another metal-braced city skyline building – the Broadgate Tower.

Looking outside the City 'box' to the north and east it is surprising how suddenly the dense, sleek City landscape melts away into the gritty borders of Brick Lane with its low-rise terraces, and the residential estates, parks and gardens around Shoreditch, Hoxton and Bethnal Green. Just beyond the concrete railway barrier sits the Boundary Street Estate, its red-brick flats with red-tiled rooftops built in the 1890s. Its streets radiate out from central Arnold Circus. That was once 'The Nichol' – an area of Shoreditch notorious for criminality and dire poverty. The pretty dreaming white spire is the top of its parish church, St Leonard's.

EAST

From the rectangular East Terrace the glass barriers surrounding its three open sides allow downward views over the City proper without having

to lean over the edge. But its 1250 square foot size is big enough to somehow mitigate vertigo. From here straight down below is Spitalfields Market, an elongated atrium that comes smack up against the white stone of Hawksmoor's Christ Church. The view of the church is partially blocked by a giant blue skyscraper built to house student residences. This is another sign of the times. Students are the next wave of immigrants settling into the East End – although they are unlikely to be driven by the poverty of their historic forebears. Further away due east, Populous's new cool blue Royal London Hospital stands out in height and colour and beyond it to the right are the

SushiSamba at the Heron Tower

towers of Canary Wharf. Beyond, to the northeast, the Olympic Park and stadium, Orbit sculpture and a wealth of new tower developments, such as Velocity, Icona Point, the Athena and the tallest – a new residential complex called 150 High Street at the crossroads by the entrance to the Olympic Park – delineate regenerated Stratford.

SOUTHEAST

From the long side of the terrace is a view just below of 1990s Beaufort House, a great post-modern bulk of grey granite with chequerboard windows housing various asset-management companies. From up

A simulation of the stunning al fresco dining experience coming to patrons of SushiSamba at the top of the Heron Tower.

The vertiginous prospect of the Gherkin, squaring up to the south terrace of the Heron Tower, with Tower Bridge in the distance to the left.

The highest outdoor cocktail in London is soon to be had from the top of the Heron Tower.

here it reveals a huge rear garden, hitherto unknown, its manicured lawns and geometric paths dotted with strange little domed neoclassical Wendy houses. It all looks so incongruous backing onto the quadrangle of raw concrete that is Petticoat Square housing estate with its brown tower, and the neighbouring narrow old market streets that surround Petticoat Lane.

SOUTH

Looking south, the Gherkin is close to this side of the terrace's glass barrier. It looks like a giant standing alongside the Heron squaring up to the super-sized Shard across the river. In between are the three blocks making up the black glass Willis Building, like a referee keeping them at arm's length.

From the short south-facing side of the rectangular terrace there is an excellent view of the City-to-be. Next to Tower 42 the new cores of the rising Pinnacle and Richard Rogers' Leadenhall Building – affectionately known as the Cheesegrater – at the crossroads of Leadenhall and Bishopsgate will soon be joining the cluster defining London's new skyline. From the top of the Heron those building sites are now dwarfed by the preparation of a site where six buildings once stood between Camomile Street and St Helen's Place. Although its footprint will be five times the Heron Tower's, fortunately it will not be tall enough to obscure the rare bird's-eye view available from here of London's oldest surviving tower complex, the Tower of London.

VERTIGO AT TOWER 42

THE CITY'S ONLY 600FT HIGH, 360-DEGREE VANTAGE POINT OPEN TO THE GENERAL PUBLIC

Vertigo is the name of the champagne bar on top of Tower 42, a landmark building in the very heart of the old City of London. Built as the NatWest Tower in 1980 and designed by Richard Seifert, the cantilevered tower was in the shape of the NatWest logo as seen from the air – although Seifert always denied that this was deliberate. Just over 600ft high, it remained the nearest London had to a skyscraper until Number One Canada Square opened in 1990. One of many buildings to suffer extensive damage from a Provisional IRA bomb in Bishopsgate in 1993, it was renamed Tower 42 after an entire recladding and interior refurbishment carried out by GMW Architects.

Address 25 Old Broad Street, London EC2N 1HQ

Nearest Tube Bank

Open To The Public? Pre-booking essential. Entrance to the tower is at street level and an escalator takes you to reception, where bookings will be checked by security.

Disabled accessibility Yes

Website www.vertigo42.co.uk

Contact details Tel 020 7877 7842

A designated enclosed lift glides upwards non-stop to Vertigo on the 42nd floor, the City's only 600ft-high vantage point with an almost 360-degree field of view that remains open to the general public. The sheer span of the capital from Vertigo's floor-to-ceiling windows is breathtaking as London radiates out in all directions almost as far as the eye can see. Some rural-looking hills to the south indicate the city's outskirts, but to the north, west and east habitation continues to the horizon. On a clear day, spot the Wembley Arch ten miles to the west, the newly regenerated Royal Docks apartment blocks six miles to the east, the Crystal Palace transmission tower eight miles to the south and Alexandra Palace set high on a hill seven miles north. Then cast your eyes straight down and from this height it is possible to re-evaluate some of those famous new Square Mile buildings.

SOUTH

From Vertigo 42's south-facing window, we get the full visual impact of Norman Foster's curvaceous black glass Willis Building on Lime Street as it steps upwards on three levels. Its shiny concave front façade is striking, with a drama and elegance that can't be fully appreciated at ground level.

Norman Foster's curved Willis Building to the left, and the blue gantries of Lloyd's of London to the rear of it, with the Thames beyond.

The cluster of chunky crystal that is Arup's Plantation Place, occupying a whole block from Fenchurch Street south to Great Tower Street, dominates like a giant's set of Rubik's cubes. Its size appears massive, yet to pedestrians it is far from intimidating. Richard Rogers' iconic Lloyd's of London on the corner of Lime and Fenchurch Streets is a giant atrium that flaunts its bits to passers-by: its transparent glass lifts, stainless steel-clad emergency stair spirals and air conditioning tubing. But from up here it looks remarkably unglamorous and utilitarian, with higgledy-piggledy rooftops of all shapes and heights straddled by bright blue gantries.

The steeply gabled neo-Gothic rooftops of architectural group GMW's pink sandstone Minster Plaza complex on Mincing Lane dominate the sightline from this window. To the west a three-storey box, a 'sky pavilion', catches the eye as it towers above the buildings at Bank Junction. This is the annexe placed by Dutch architect Rem Koolhaas on top of his new steel and glass cube, the banking headquarters of Rothschild in New Court. From the window that overlooks the east, just a stone's throw away, sits the now-iconic Gherkin

From up here the Thames turns sepia in the spring sunshine and glitters as it holds the outline reflections of the buildings lining each bank. At ground level the river's current would obscure this amazing surface pattern, but at this height it is an astonishing vista that few Londoners know exists.

Across the river in Southwark on the south bank, the trains that continually arrive at and depart from London's main stations morph into silent snakes, appearing and disappearing as they curl between the buildings. The leaning glass globe of Norman Foster's City Hall, home to the Mayor and the London Assembly, sits overlooking the Thames on green Potters Park next to Tower Bridge like a ball waiting to be kicked, while the Shard protrudes above the south side of London Bridge.

WEST

From the west-facing windows, it comes as a pleasant surprise to see how so many of the City's older office-block roofs have been pierced by domes and glass atria of various shapes. And how many flat roofs have been developed into colourful landscaped private retreats for hard-working occupants below. One that stands out is Foggo Associates' Drapers' Gardens – a three-layered glass and steel development on Throgmorton Street just behind the Bank of England. Each of the three rooftop terraces is thickly planted

with wild-looking shrubs and hedges, creating a 246ft-high pocket park with overhanging foliage softening the building's angular glass edges.

To the right, Finsbury Circus is not round but ellipsoid. Further away, the roof of the British Museum's Great Court is not 3312 panels of computer-designed glass shapes but an undulating green pillow.

NORTH AND EAST

In the distance the white roof of the Emirates Stadium acts as a perfect foil for the green splash of Hampstead Heath, a vast expanse of wild parkland rising on a hill above the rows of north London residences. To the east the clusters of trees of Victoria Park frame the Hackney edge of the Olympic Park.

East from Tower 42: the Gherkin with the skyscrapers of Canary Wharf in the distance.

THE GHERKIN OR 30 ST MARY AXE

A TRANQUIL HAVEN IN THE SKY FROM WHICH TO VIEW 360 DEGREES OF LONDON

Foster and Partners built Swiss Re's UK headquarters in 2003 on the site of the Baltic Exchange. Its energy-efficient 40-storey cylindrical shape has become an icon defining the London skyline. The shape stops air currents sweeping around the base causing discomforting whirlwinds. When the building changed hands in 2007, it was renamed after its address, 30 St Mary Axe, but it is usually referred to as the Gherkin. The club on the 40th floor, with its Searcy's restaurant and bar, is currently the highest in London. The lifts float up to the 36th floor at a rate of 20ft per second, while two further separate lifts transfer guests from there to the 39th floor restaurant. But go up the last staircase and step into the 40th floor bar to marvel at a tableau of London from the sky.

Address 30 St Mary Axe, EC3A 8EP
Nearest Tube Aldgate
Open To The Public? Members only
Disabled accessibility Yes
Website www.30stmaryaxe.com
Contact details 020 7071 5009

With a 360-degree view under the lens of the building (the only piece of curved glass on the Gherkin's façade, forming the apex) it feels as if the senses are drawn into a world apart. Up here, 525 feet above London, hermetically sealed off from life below, it is an eerie, soundless experience of city life. From this tranquil haven in the sky (or in the clouds on rainy days), the familiar hectic rush below looks like a play unfolding.

The view is unimpeded, so wherever you choose to sit or stand it feels as if London is in your grip. Architects, planners and engineers could leave the virtual GPS modelling behind and come up here to assess what impact new constructions might have on London's skyline. This view presents the biggest picture. Seeing it all gives a curious and dangerous feeling of empowerment.

NORTHEAST

With the 2012 Games almost upon us, the Olympic Park is a fine orientation point from which to start a panoramic tour. Within the Park the divisions and connections between venues, village and warm-up areas are visible, making perfect sense of

North-westwards from the Gherkin, with the BT Tower far left, and Wembley Stadium distant right.

the whole. Moreover, this view gives a perfect opportunity to digest how profound the effects of regeneration have been on east London. The capital has marched eastwards, dislodging the West End from its role as the centre. Now that the crane forests are thinning out, Stratford's growth from the docks up to Westfield Stratford is apparent. Office and residential towers and landscaped housing estates of all heights – including the new Nido Student Living building in Spitalfields, the Royal London Hospital extension in Whitechapel and the tower of 150 High Street in Stratford itself – are well incorporated into the old East End fabric.

This vantage point reveals the true scale and proportion of what regeneration in the 1980s and 1990s by the London Docklands Development Corporation achieved. Here we are above the usual blind spots created by the River Thames' curves. It zigzags alongside Bermondsey, Rotherhithe and

Deptford – all sites of ongoing reconstruction projects. At Greenwich just beyond we even get a fine view all the way to the grand Royal Observatory on top of the highest point of Greenwich Park and the pepperpot towers of the Royal Naval College down by the water's edge. Post Big Bang, the swathe of Canary Wharf towers on the uppermost part of the Isle of Dogs peninsula became a symbol of London's leading role in international finance, replacing the old images of the City of London used to illustrate financial stories on the nightly TV news.

NORTH

In the foreground just below us, the A10 (the old Roman-built Ermine Street, discernible in satellite shots of the UK), named Bishopsgate at this point, looks especially prominent.

It is a wonder that the preserved medieval city grid pattern that splays out from it remains perfectly intact as the City accommodates more and more daringly shaped high-rise additions. The elegantly skinny 755ft Heron Tower that stands so close by looks like an ultra-futuristic stack of vertical three-storey village units. To the west of the A10 the roof of the Emirates Stadium, perched in Islington, appears from this angle to be practically in contact with the Heron's west flank. Amazingly, the view west includes Harrow on the Hill on the horizon, fully 16 miles away.

The Tower of London and Tower Bridge, to the southeast of the Gherkin.

'Like the nosecone of a fabulous airship': how the Guardian's *Jonathan Glancey described the bar at the top of the Gherkin.*

WEST

Between St Paul's Cathedral and the Gherkin there is a unique view of the City's newest office and retail complex, One New Change. From up here the sharp 'nose' and 'wings' of the 'stealth bomber' suddenly stand out as clear as day. A crazy feature also not really visible at street level is its creased elevations, which make the whole structure appear like an unfolding origami plane. Even more weird, on the Cheapside-facing wing a patch of red roof reflects downwards onto the side of the building like an autumn-coloured vine, once again invisible at ground level.

Down at the Bank Junction end of Cheapside, the streaky brown and pink of One, Poultry's façade makes a surprisingly sharp colour contrast to the grey stone colonnaded 'temples' around it. Its triangular flatiron shape with wings looks from this angle like a beached ship, but more impressive is the great view of its roof gardens (a fashion first for the City when it opened in 1997) in crescent, circular and triangular shapes.

The Gherkin or 30 St Mary Axe

THE MONUMENT

THE OLDEST SURVIVING MAN–MADE VIEWING POINT IN LONDON, PRESENTING A BROAD–BRUSH CHALLENGE BETWEEN TWO OF LONDON'S MOST INFLUENTIAL ARCHITECTS

The Monument was built 11 years after Parliament decreed that the Great Fire of 1666 should be given a memorial. There are 311 steps up the inside of this fluted Doric column to an outside viewing gallery below the gilt bronze flaming urn at the top. It reaches just over 200ft, the exact distance between its entrance and the baker's premises in Pudding Lane where the Great Fire broke out. All four sides of its plinth are inscribed to recall in Latin and English and in sculptural allegory the history of the Great Fire and the rebuilding of London and its spirit afterwards. In 2007, when the Monument and its surrounding public space were redesigned, an inscribed memorial stone to scientist Robert Hooke was at last placed at the column's foot to rectify historical neglect and the lie that this was entirely the work of architect Christopher Wren.

Address Located at junction of Monument Street and Fish Street Hill

Nearest Tube Monument

Open To The Public? 9:30am–17:30pm daily; entry charge

Disabled accessibility No

Website www.themonument.info

Contact details 020 7626 2717

The point of climbing the Monument today is to reach the oldest surviving man-made viewing point in London. Looking down from a four-sided gallery cage, not many sights or sites remain from the era in which it was built, but this view of the capital has fascinated Londoners for over 300 years. In the City itself only the Thames, the churches and a handful of old institutions like the Guildhall survive. But the biggest difference is surely on the horizon. Beyond the old square mile, Wren and Hooke would have been able to spot the rural villages of Hampstead, Kensington, Stratford-at-Bow or Peckham on a clear day. Although their lives are separated by some 350 years, the view today sets up a broad-brush challenge between two of London's most influential architects: Christopher Wren and Norman Foster.

SOUTH

The river immediately below is almost as wide as in Wren's day, although its mud-coloured flow has accelerated over the years with each new bridge with piers that has been installed.

From up here today the river looks strange: the sight of London Bridge has been entirely obscured, partly by the clock tower of St Magnus the Martyr, one of Wren's 40 or so post-Great Fire rebuilds, but mostly by the adjacent massive white stone bulk of Adelaide House with its Egyptian-style roof overhang.

Following the curve of the river as it flows east, the eye is drawn to the south bank where Norman Foster's architectural designs reign supreme. The 1980s regeneration of the old docks by the southern end of London Bridge demolished swathes of Victorian offices but left the lively, original façades of riverfront warehouses and refits. The grimly serious brick-fronted Southwark Crown Court is side by side with Foster and Partners' More London development – a dense series of pier-shaped glass towers set back from a luxuriously wide walkway dotted with sculptures. The charcoal-grey paved amphitheatre known as the Scoop stands between these and the smooth bulging front, like a discarded giant's headlamp, of Foster's City Hall. Perhaps Wren would have appreciated its architectural subtleties – especially its forward-tilting, shallow-domed roof. Its photovoltaic panels, visible only from up here, power the pumps below ground level that operate the building's cooling system from its own borehole.

EAST

From the east-facing balcony, look over Tower Bridge and the four turrets of the White Tower (restored by Wren for Charles II) peer over the top of the two gentle curved white rooftops of Norman Foster's Tower Place complex next to the Tower of London's entrance plaza. Just in front of this double linked pavilion

East from the Monument, with HMS Belfast in the foreground.

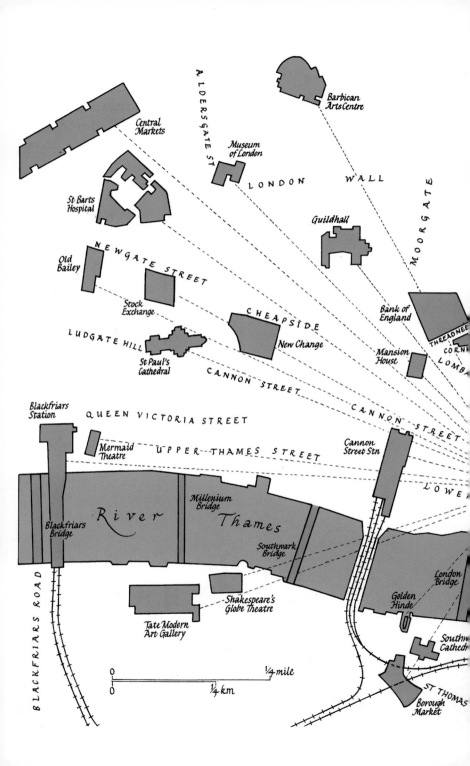

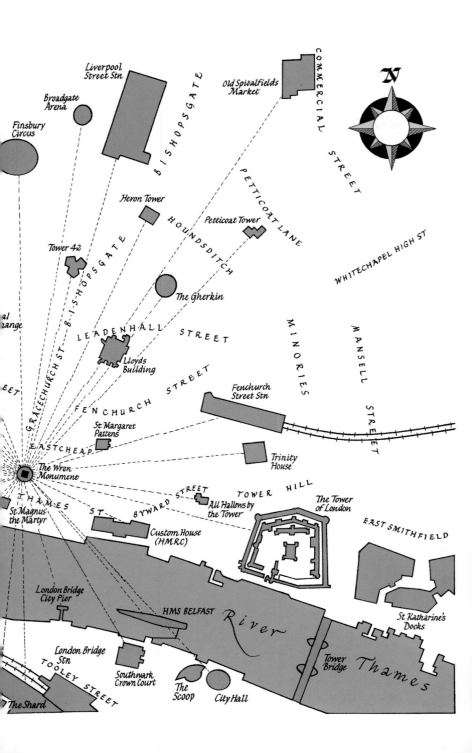

roof is an unusual close-up view of a quirky Wren-designed white stone buttressed spire, open at its base. It shoots up just a stone's throw away from the Monument's gallery beside the green copper spire of All Hallows by the Tower; although impossible to identify as such from up here, this is all that remains of Wren's rebuilt St Dunstan's in the East after the body of the church was destroyed in the Blitz. Neighbouring St Margaret Pattens' square white tower with four pinnacles has a lead-covered timber spire and gilded vane clearly presented at this height. The records show that Wren rebuilt this tiny parish church at a cost of £5000, and a monogrammed pew inside indicates that it may have been the church where he regularly worshipped.

NORTH

From the north-facing gallery, the elegant triple-scooped structure of Foster and Partners' newest distinctive skyline landmark – the UK headquarters of insurance giant

Looking north: from centre to right, the Heron Tower, Gherkin and Willis Building.

Willis, known as the Willis Building – separates into three heights, the tallest being 28 storeys. Stepping up skywards, each concave block curves into the one behind, all in black reflective glass and a stunning addition from up here. The Willis Building dwarfs its neighbours, including the barrel-roofed atrium of Lloyd's of London next door, commonly acknowledged as the building that broke the mould of Square Mile architecture. Once Richard Rogers' Cheesegrater is finished, the battle of the City towers will recommence.

WEST

The rounded Gherkin is still the most attention-grabbing skyline building that Norman Foster has ever built for London. But in this direction it's the dome of St Paul's Cathedral that completes a Foster v. Wren London skyline.

CITY HALL

A TALE OF TWO CITIES

A new government for London with its own mayor in the new millennium required a new home. Architects Foster and Partners created London's most ecologically sound building in shape and angle to minimise the necessity for air conditioning. So successful was the concept, it was taken several stages further in the design of the Gherkin a few years later. The choice of glass as building material symbolised the intended transparency of style of future London governments. The building quickly became a popular, if somewhat controversial, new skyline attraction on the south bank of the Thames, stealing attention from the Tower of London and Tower Bridge. It was also a beacon signalling the long-awaited rebuild of the south bank between Tower and London Bridges.

Address The Queen's Walk, SE1 2AA
Nearest Tube London Bridge
Open To The Public? Mon-Thurs 8:30am-6pm, Fri 8:30am-5:30pm
Disabled accessibility Yes
Website www.london.gov.uk
Contact details 020 7983 4000

The view from the top, circular terrace of City Hall, though not accessible for a full 360 degrees, clearly defines London as a tale of two cities – north and south. From this gentle height the personality of the capital could not look more split by the River Thames. Facing north, on the river bank from right to left we see the ancient Tower of London, an empty building site, a 1970s stepped concrete block, the early 19th-century Customs House with trees in front and its late 19th-century neighbour, old Billingsgate Fish Market.

From this height the glass complex of Tower Place, designed by Norman Foster, sits on the next layer behind. But then the City buildings rise up into one great steep mountain ridge of varying stone and glass blocking all views beyond.

In contrast, when you walk 180 degrees around to the south side of City Hall's terrace, you see a low-rise London that lets you view as far as ten miles south. Looking like an entirely separate city, it has nothing in common with the London you have just seen to the north. Londoners often define themselves as being either from north or south of the river, as if that pinpointed some essential social difference. The view from up here would support the concept that there is indeed a huge geographical and hence historical divide.

The firmer geological structure of the land on the north bank and the river's propensity to flood on the south explain why, two thousand years ago, London developed originally on the north bank alone. Until about 130 years ago everything to the south was officially Surrey and did not even call itself London. The south bank is the traditional home of the industries that served the capital.

The north bank: a Thames Clipper docks at Tower Pier pontoon near the hectic heart of the City.

SOUTH

From this side of the terrace we overlook Bermondsey – a good example of London's industrial legacy and once a dockside hub where beer, leather, vinegar, jam, hats, pots, paper and biscuits were manufactured alongside the homes of people who worked in those factories. The railway is still there but Bermondsey's industrial legacy has disappeared, leaving a low-lying expanse of land with no iconic high-rise financial buildings. On the contrary, the

contaminating tanning pits and potteries have given way to spacious parks, new low-rise residential complexes, retrofitted factories and market buildings – still in keeping with the historical urban terrain, but on a human scale.

Directly below City Hall is Potters Park, and adjacent to it a chunk of prime real estate at the entrance of Tower Bridge awaiting purely residential development – impossible to imagine that happening at the other end of the bridge. A mile or

so south of that empty site we see where the once fashionable 18th-century Bermondsey Spa was taken over by industry in the 19th century. It is just a small part of Southwark's massive 50-acre regeneration of low-density, low-rise, affordable and private housing estates. From a glance across the area of Southwark it is obvious from the proliferation of parks, schools and playing fields that local amenities were prioritised when regeneration began some 25 years ago. The 1920s white art deco Alaska Factory stands out with its red neon name on Grange Road by Bermondsey Spa Gardens. Once a centre for working seal fur, it is now converted into private flats, as is the cherry-red-brick Hartley Jam factory just in front and to the right of it, the top of its old chimney stack just visible. Beyond, just over nine miles to the south, is the Crystal Palace transmission tower.

NORTH

Bear that view in mind when you walk back to the northern side of the terrace. Crossing any Thames bridge in the City from south to north and you are sucked into the hectic heart of the world's largest international financial centre. Medieval street grid patterns are lost amid stone, concrete and glass high-rises such as Plantation Place, Minster Court and the Barbican. The only reminder that humans ever actually lived in the poky Square Mile is the number of churches that remain. On the north bank we see the

20 Fenchurch Street (the Walkie-Talkie) will soon rival the Gherkin on the northern skyline.

tightest conglomeration of landmark buildings to be found anywhere in the country, including Tower 42, the Gherkin and, still a work in progress, Raphael Vinoly's 20 Fenchurch Street. This view questions what we actually cherish about our heritage.

A grand view of Tower Bridge to the east of City Hall.

However, all is changing on the two sides of the Thames. Invisible from up here, many a ground floor of the City's new and refitted old buildings are given over to health clubs, hair and beauty shops, coffee shops and grocers. Even a new local butcher has found retail City space.

SOUTHWEST

Now walk to the left-hand corner, where 40 degrees of the circular terrace is blocked off. To the extreme left we see, poking out above the roofline of neighbouring More London Riverside, the Shard. London's – and Europe's – tallest new building, containing offices, a hotel and apartments up to its 65th floor, is the harbinger of change. There it stands on the south bank of London Bridge with its new neighbour The Place going up beside it. It is a signal that it may not be long before the two Londons north and south of the river become one.

TOWER BRIDGE EXHIBITION WALKWAY

A UNIQUE BIRD'S-EYE VIEW OF LONDON FROM THE MIDDLE OF THE THAMES

Tower Bridge, London's iconic bridge, is famous for its opening bascules. They prioritise access for Thames waterway traffic into the Pool of London while providing vital connectivity across the Thames for vehicles and pedestrians on two separate levels. In the late 19th century, City Surveyor and architect Horace Jones designed this masterpiece of engineering to solve dense congestion on London Bridge and the Thames. The walkway bridges high above the vehicle traffic were a great attraction from which to view London but were otherwise a failure and closed in 1910. With no lifts in those days, working people – usually laden with baggage – preferred to risk the traffic and cross at road level rather than climb and descend the staircases in the towers at either end. In 1982 the walkways were covered and reopened to the public.

Address Tower Bridge Road, SE1 2UP
Nearest Tube Tower Hill
Open To The Public? Summer 10am–6pm, Winter 9:30am-5:30pm; entry charge
Disabled accessibility Yes
Website www.towerbridge.org.uk
Contact details 020 7403 3761

The Tower Bridge Walkway, 138ft above the bridge's road, is the only place that offers a bird's-eye view of London from the middle of the Thames. The downstream walkway overlooks the Thames as it flows eastwards past its old docks and industrial banks – the sort of back door of London. When you transfer to the upstream walkway all the glamour of London's fair icons distract from the river. But from either side the view is all about the Thames, and the Thames is the acknowledged key to understanding London.

Although there are no more surge tides thanks to the Thames Barrier downstream at Silvertown, the hostile swell and fall of the murky brown water below is mesmerising. Strongly tidal, with a 21ft difference between high and low tide, the river offers an alluringly unpredictable view. Like London itself, on any chosen day, you never know what you are going to experience looking down on the Thames from here. The influence of weather and light create potentially

Westwards, upriver, from Tower Bridge.

the water immediately below and those pleasure boats are in for a choppy ride the moment the tide starts to turn. All the stories about the dangers of its strong currents and freezing temperatures suddenly seem highly plausible. Living on the old Wapping or Bermondsey dockside in one of those delightfully restored warehouses with a balcony where the loopholes once were would be a different story, but what can be the attraction that lures anyone to live on a houseboat in London?

huge visual differences. But it's the inevitable tidal fluctuations twice a day that transform the river's personality as much as its appearance. One moment the water seems shallow and benign, revealing expanses of gravelly shoreline. Here and there cormorants paddle waiting for the tide to change, bringing shoals of food. People have climbed down the embankment and are dotted around the foreshore scanning for 'treasure', while hooting pleasure boats with waving passengers slice through the central stretch of water, leaving those lines of house barges moored on the north bank at Wapping and on the south at Bermondsey gently swaying.

Return another time, another day and the river looks as if it is racing ferociously to fill up the embankments before reaching high tide, when it has to change direction again. The river swirls menacingly around the piers of the bridge in

EAST

The downstream walkway is not high enough for the Thames to be visible as it reappears beyond the sharp curve at Wapping – although it is possible to glimpse Greenwich Observatory and the towers of Greenwich Palace on the skyline. But one or two river-related literary gems can be appreciated at this height. On the south bank, between the white building of the Design Museum and the riverbank where the houseboats are moored, is an inlet. That is St Saviour's Dock, and the land next to it is known as Jacob's Island. In Charles Dickens's *Oliver Twist*, this swampy patch of land, un-embanked in those days and regularly flooded by the unforgiving Thames, was the grisly place where Bill Sikes lived and where he and his girl Nancy died in horrible circumstances.

Staying with the south bank, but going east, is the riverbank that

Tower Bridge Exhibition Walkway

Samuel Pepys refers to in his diary, describing how he would save the shilling ferry fee from the City and walk his way to the Deptford shipyards along the Thames. As the river curves we see Rotherhithe and Cherry Garden Pier, the very spot where Pepys would stop off for some drinking on his way home.

WEST

The view from the bridge's sister walkway facing west offers the drama of a new piece of public realm on the south bank by City Hall. It can be seen from up here how the More London development has reworked the narrow dockside alleys and old grid-pattern streets for the crowds milling around between the bulge of City Hall, the Crown Court and the row of sparkling glass pier-shaped offices along the new embankment. In the midst of it all is the Scoop – this swirl of a shallow open amphitheatre is a new take on the old public entertainment spaces that have characterised the south bank since Shakespeare's time. With the Shard's breathtaking glass height rising behind, there is a Lilliputian comic edge to this perspective.

Looking across to the north bank, the Tower of London's crenellate curtain walls are layered like an onion, with visitors walking on their ramparts. Further to the west, the riverbank is dotted with a row of towers: the Monument, the dome of St Paul's, the BT Tower, Centre Point. As the river curves sharply it disappears from sight, north and south bank merging into a single westward view.

Beyond the Mississippi Queen paddlesteamer is the white Design Museum, and then St Saviour's Dock with houseboat moorings beyond.

PLATEAU AT CANADA PLACE

A CLOSE-UP VIEW OF THE NEW LONDON

Canada Place is that low-rise building swathed in wavy glass on the east side of Canada Square. Plateau, its top storey restaurant, bar and grill, sits on the fourth floor above one of Canary Wharf's three underground shopping arcades. Below are Waitrose and the Reebok Sports Club. Plateau's restaurant and grill tables are arranged to place diners at all angles to the double-height picture window that runs uninterrupted the full length of its west-facing façade. In winter, the temporary outdoor skating rink on Canada Square just below takes centre stage. With blue sparkling lights in the surrounding trees it is a pleasant reminder that the concept of Canary Wharf with its North American names was brought to London by Canadians.

Address Canada Place, E14 5ER
Nearest Tube Canary Wharf
Open To The Public? Prior booking needed
Disabled accessibility Yes
Website www.plateau-restaurant.co.uk
Contact details 020 7715 7100

There is something rare about a London view like this. Hemmed in, it provides neither geographic nor historic references to the city. From about 60ft above ground there is not a single landmark to identify a sense of place. There is no clue to be had from just a couple of visible brand names like Citigroup or Bank of America tacked onto buildings. Austere and pristine, this view is so stripped of definition we could be in any one of a multitude of places. Without skies above or houses below, there is a perversely dehumanised charm to this view.

From Plateau the view is all about reflections. Built on the site of West India Dock, constructed in the very early 19th century to regulate and protect trade in sugar, rum and molasses, the new Canary Wharf has fully taken over the mantle of the Wharf's past. But that is only one kind of reflection from here. The Canary Wharf icon of Number One Canada Square, just a few metres opposite Plateau, becomes an impenetrable, geometrically patterned window blind shielding the view from the perspective beyond.

To the right, on the north side of Canada Square, those awe-inspiring giant office towers – the HSBC

The Christmas ice rink in Canada Square: an entirely modern view of London.

Tower and Bank of America – obscure the view of the water and original warehouses of West India Import Dock. In the late 1980s Canary Wharf's development synchronised with the City's Big Bang and an explosion of new markets and trading activity. The new towers seemed to symbolise a fresh era of freedom, but the north block of Canada Square also housed (and still does) the Financial Services Authority, which ironically ushered in a new age of compliance and regulations governing and often stymying the financial markets.

Looking down so close to Canary Wharf's street level, the atmosphere seems somehow rarefied, as if it has physically and mentally detached itself from everything else happening in London. Unless you can access the higher echelons of any of its towers you will not gain a view outside its confines either.

Public realm it is not. It is a privately owned and managed zone, as metal plates on strategic posts and corners remind its workforce and visitors. Its pristine litter-free streets permit the matt charcoal-grey pavements all around to complement the shiny grey steel and glass triple-height foyers inside those perfectly aligned grids of office tower entrances. Plateau's modest height pulls the viewer right into the heart of this monochromatic world, where groups of figures look as if they have been deliberately posited in landscapes at the foot of flagship buildings representing global canopied service stations around it virtually obliterate all but a slice of green lawn on Canada Square. Just the tiniest touch of branding red on the logos of BankAmerica, HSBC and the umbrella of Citigroup provides disproportionate relief. From here a narrow strip of rust-red panel just visible between buildings on the external façade of the Docklands Light Railway station is a joy – as are the double yellow 'no parking' lines along every road.

High-rise skyline views in the right places can truly liberate the senses. Here, the crowding presence of so many vast towers rising so high and so close means that to avoid the goldfish bowl effect, you must look straight up through Plateau's glass ceiling, not down, to achieve a sense of freedom.

On a day of unbroken winter clouds, their pale grisaille reflections bounce off the opaque glass-walled buildings all around Canada Square, causing a sort of blanket whiteout. This can grow exponentially as white reflects white on white in white all around. On a sunny day, even when the blue of the sky reflects off the surrounding glass and stainless steel façades and the mature trees that line Canada Square are in full leaf, Canary Wharf is still strangely and intensely impersonal for a London neighbourhood. But from up here at least it looks a little less like an architect's computer-generated image.

One Canada Square glittering after dark from Plateau.

enterprises like Thomson Reuters or Barclays.

Grey, black, shiny black, white and silver – probably even the dock river rats are not allowed to be brown. Where occasional colour seeps through it becomes blindingly exquisite by contrast. In winter the white ice skating rink and white-

Plateau at Canada Place

50

ATTIC PAN PENINSULA

THE ISLE OF DOGS AND BEYOND – A LANDSCAPE TRANSFORMED

Attic, the highest residents' bar in Europe, is on the 48th floor of Pan Peninsula – the sleek residential development in South Quay over the South Dock from Canary Wharf. It was built over part of the old Enterprise Zone that helped kick-start regeneration of this zone on the Isle of Dogs 30 years ago.

Address Canary Wharf, E14 9HN
Nearest Tube South Quay DLR
Open To The Public? The two Pan Peninsula towers are private but Attic is open to all, subject to pre-booking, Tuesday to Saturday from 5 p.m. Entrance is via Tompkins, the ground floor Pan Peninsula restaurant by the DLR station.
Disabled accessibility Yes
Website www.theatticbar.co.uk
Contact details 020 8305 3080

On the north side the view from Attic is virtually cut off by the tall towers of Canada Square. This is the side of London's regeneration showpiece that has always grabbed the limelight. Above bird's-eye height, however, the floor-to-ceiling south-facing windows present the unsung Isle of Dogs; the view summarises a far-reaching change in fortune that has affected thousands. Just a few years ago it would have been unrealistic to think this peninsula – once a tough and isolated industrial backyard – could be so utterly transformed.

SOUTH

Looking south, the geography of the Isle becomes clear. Just over a mile in length and half a mile wide, the 'L' shaped Millwall Dock, an expanse of water that runs down the centre and to the west, is preserved. So are the green expanses of Mudchute and Millwall Parks to the southeast of the dock. The Thames shore, where once the Industrial Revolution brought shipbuilding and its associated industries, is now built up instead with acres of new homes, allowing access to the riverfront for the first time in centuries.

The advantage of this viewpoint is an unusual insider's peek at the land alongside Millwall's Inner Dock. Halfway down the dock's water channel is a Dutch-style swing bridge called Glengall Bridge, and in the distance the terraces of homes on the south side can be seen, the old cranes still in situ.

Beyond, Island Gardens, right at the river's edge on the southern tip,

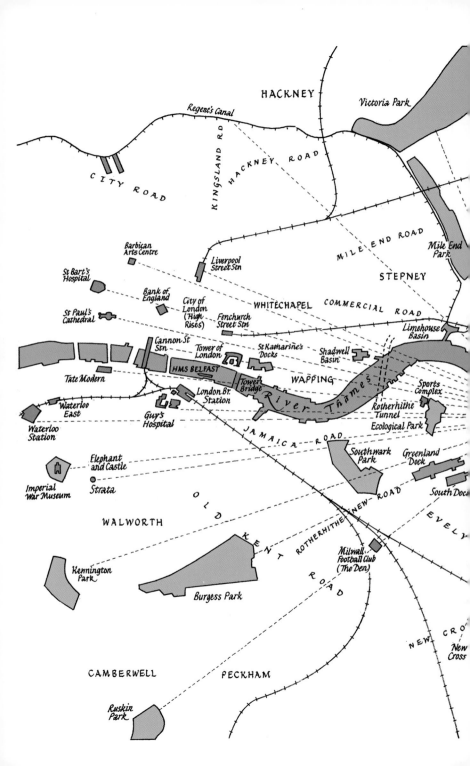

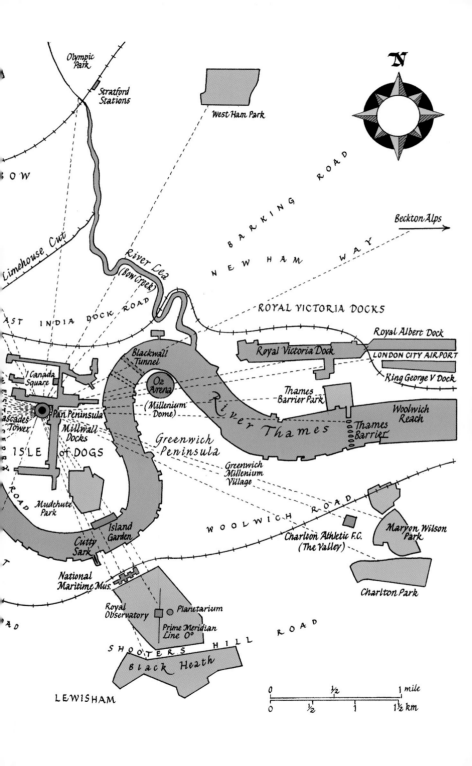

A close encounter of the third kind with the O₂, landed across the Thames from Pan Peninsula.

stares straight across the Thames at the four symmetrical buildings of white stone with majestic twin pepperpot towers that made up the old Royal Naval College at Greenwich. The view from here, with the Queen's House white and solitary against the colonnade and steep green hill leading up to the Royal Observatory behind, is more impressive even than that painted by Canaletto from this spot 250 years ago.

EAST

Turning to Pan Peninsula's east front, there is a great view of the original entry gates to West India Quay South Dock, still intact and connected to the Preston Road (which runs down the Isle's eastern side) by a clunking jetty drawbridge that is rarely opened for passing vessels these days.

The silver-white roofed O_2 Arena, the world's largest covered structure, with the yellow antennae that support its fabric dome, looks disconcertingly close on the Greenwich peninsula. Meanwhile, the view exposes acres of construction right behind it; on the south bank, among a tangle of red cranes, the Emirates Air Line cable car station and associated masts is taking shape. This new cable car, crossing the Thames in just five minutes with gondola cabins arriving every 30 seconds, will be ready by summer 2012.

Beyond Greenwich is an unusual glimpse of the Thames as it straightens itself out on a stretch past Woolwich. The six silver piers of the Thames Barrier catch the sunlight, looking like a line of elegant sailing ships lined up under starter's orders for a race to the Estuary.

To the left, nearer to us on the river's north bank, there is a bird sanctuary and marina in the old Blackwall Basin, originally dug out to hold cargo vessels waiting to unload at the West India Docks. The Basin is the only barrier to a continuous line of encroaching development on Harbour Quay coming down from Canary Wharf. Next to it is Wood Wharf, with an 'L'-shaped expanse of grey tarmac jutting out into the dock water reserved as a landing pad for helicopters and small aircraft.

WEST

From the windows facing due west can be seen a few 19th-century streets that survive between here and the Thames, alongside new housing off the main Westferry Road which skirts the peninsula on this side. The Isle here once housed food-processing factories like McDougall's Self Raising Flour, Maconochie's Pan-Yan Pickles and Morton's Confectionery. Between Westferry Road and the Thames we can see John McDougall Gardens, named after a family member who worked for the LCC here. Traditionally the cleaner, more residential side of the Isle, it clearly remains so, with new tower blocks and estates inland stretching out as far as the river's edge. A few tree-lined streets maintain the old names like Manilla, Malabar and Cuba.

Across the Thames lie Rotherhithe's old housing estates alongside the new Harmsworth Printing works at Surrey Docks and the spreading metallic roofs of Canada Water's shopping centre. With Bermondsey and Southwark beyond, there is a stunning low-rise skyline view all the way to Elephant and Castle with the profile of the Strata, the Gherkin-style landmark of Walworth, its 43 floors rising above everything else.

Near London Bridge the Shard twinkles like a huge crystal wand in the sky, catching the sun by day and lit up by night. Just below it, from this angle the glass bulge of City Hall juts out over the river. The glass piers of More London line up along the Jubilee Walkway, highlighting the blue-painted ironwork and grey stone frame of Tower Bridge. From Attic on a clear day Wembley Arch may shine nine miles away, but the much nearer riverbank of the Pool of London steals the limelight.

A cool, neon-lit venue for a skyline drink with magnificent views out over south and east London.

HOLDEN POINT

FROM WASTELAND TO OLYMPIC PARK: THE VIEWPOINT THAT CLINCHED THE GAMES

Until seven years ago Holden Point was an anonymous 21-storey local authority block of flats. But in 2005 officials from the International Olympic Committee (IOC) went up to its open rooftop to overlook Stratford's neglected railway lands and the acres of derelict, contaminated land that lay all around. The skyline beyond, with the City of London, the West End and Canary Wharf to the west and the O2 Arena, ExCeL and City Airport to the southeast, was a revelation to them. Much closer to central London and other potential sites than they had imagined, this massive brownfield site was ripe for the development of an Olympic and Paralympic Park. The view clinched the IOC's decision to choose London's bid to stage the 2012 Games. Since then thousands of people, from local schoolchildren to the Queen, have visited what is now an indoor viewing gallery on Holden Point's roof.

Address Waddington Road, E15 1QN
Nearest Tube Stratford
Open daily to pre-arranged groups
Disabled accessibility Yes
Website www.opvg.co.uk
Contact details 020 3373 0421

 In July 2005, the criss-crossing railway tracks and the tributaries of the River Lea running through the site were the only points of orientation from the viewing gallery. Now we overlook from Holden Point a restored quarter of ancient London complete with new postcode (E20), new locality names and a new transport network.

WEST

The most stunning view is to the west. Immediately below, outside the perimeter of the Olympic Park, is the local housing estate with its popular Railway Tavern, with several light industrial buildings immediately to the right. Beyond the temporary barriers around this side of the site, temporary white tented structures amid huge expanses of tarmac mark the entry points for ticketholders coming to the test events held since early 2011.

Further beyond, the light brown walls running east–west mark where the Eurostar tracks and the new High Speed One railway line between Kent and St Pancras emerge, having passed through the Park entirely

The towers of the City form a backdrop to the Olympic stadium and the Westfield shopping mall.

underground. These tracks divide the view in the middle distance, with the athletes' village to the right and the new shopping and transport complex of Westfield Stratford to the left. A couple of bridges span the track, but the building over the railway with pale green glass walls in front of a great white arch is the new Stratford International station. On the left alongside the tracks sits Westfield Stratford's shiny three-storey brass tiled façade, the red logos on its sides flagging up its identity.

Stratford's new bus station is to the front, and before it the new Energy Centre with tall 'L'-shaped chimney. If the day is clear enough it is possible to see its twin on the park's western edge, built to service the Games

venues. Close by, it is also possible to see the rectangular low-rise building, faced in dark copper, that is the Handball Arena. Behind the blue-green glass office tower adjacent to the station rises the tangled red tubing of Anish Kapoor's Orbit, sitting next to the main Olympic Stadium. Another of the three tall hotels on the Westfield Stratford site – this one built of contrasting brownish-grey stone with white-framed windows – virtually conceals the view of the stadium itself. Just a curve of the venue's upper perimeter with its distinctive white triangular lighting towers is visible.

Back to that rectangular blue-green glass office block, by the far corner on the left a new rust-coloured steel

West from Holden Point as the Olympic Park is laid out. To the right is the Athletes' Village.

footbridge spans the local East Anglia tracks and the Central Line to link Stratford Regional station, a capital 'D'-shaped glass building on the other side of the tracks, with Westfield Stratford. Across the bridge, the building with off-white façade next to the Westfield transport hub, with logo just visible, is Marks and Spencer – the anchor store at the eastern end of the mall. At the other (west) end

a Premier Inn hotel sits on top of the mall next to John Lewis, the western end anchor store.

The Athletes' Village is on raised ground alongside the East Anglia-bound railway track. From here we can only see a fraction of the 11 village hubs, each designed by a different architect. The high-rise blocks in each hub will be home to 17,000 athletes and organisers during the Olympics and Paralympics; refitted afterwards, they will become 2,800 family homes, part of the new

The Athletes' Village near completion.

London district of Chobham Manor. On the right-hand side, beside a road bridge across the railway tracks, sits a low-rise white block that will be a polyclinic for the new residents; the distinguished turquoise and white glass circular building just behind that will become Chobham Academy, the new local school.

Just behind the tallest building at the back of the village hub, poking out on either side, are two tiny parts of the bright white basketball arena. At the right-hand edge of the last housing block, an ellipsoidal white wing seems to jut from the side and back. That is the one of the elegant curves of the Velodrome on the northwestern side of the Park. The man-made humped landscape of the BMX track is just visible beside it on the right.

Two outdoor hockey and tennis arenas to the right of the cycling facilities have been constructed with tiers of fixed seating either side of a low tan-brown building that houses the indoor tennis courts. The white tents behind are the temporary training pools for swimming, diving and water polo. Behind them, outside the park's western perimeter, can be seen the three white and blue peaked roofs of Spitalfields Market, which moved out of Bishopsgate to Leyton in the early 1990s.

Further beyond the park, looking due west the skyline offers an uninterrupted view of central London's signature buildings. To the

left in the distance are Canary Wharf's towers, and closer the silhouettes of residential tower blocks under construction. The Gherkin, the Shard, the Heron Tower, the London Eye, St Paul's, Broadgate Tower and the BT Tower all look from this distance as if they live next door to each other. To the right, the hills of Hampstead, Highgate and Alexandra Palace mark the northerly limits to the view.

SOUTH

The south-facing window of Holden Point's viewing gallery should not be neglected. The white tubular triangles on the roof of the ExCeL convention centre stand out on a sunny day, as do the yellow spikes above the O_2 Arena on the opposite bank of the Thames. Further to the south, Shooters Hill delineates the skyline.

Alexandra Palace high on its hill to the northwest from Holden Point.

THE ROYAL VICTORIA DOCK BRIDGE

A MAGNIFICENT NEW MAN-MADE VIEW OF DOCKLANDS REGENERATION

Designed by architects Lifschutz Davidson for the London Docklands Development Corporation and opened in 1999, this footbridge looks like a giant sailing craft wedged between the north and south sides of the dock. Although privately owned, it is in fact the first suspended walkway in London open to the public. The dock itself was opened by Prince Albert in 1855, the first of three that became known locally as 'The Royals'. By the end of the 1970s, vast container ships had rendered London's docks redundant. The Royal Victoria was one of the last to close.

Address Western Gateway, E16
Nearest Tube Custom House DLR
Open to the public? Yes
Disabled accessibility Yes

The footbridge from Victoria Dock station was built to provide access between the north and south sides of the dock, but its construction has coincidentally afforded Londoners a magnificent new man-made view of London. Walk onto the pontoon and go up to the bridge, either by taking one of the two lifts or by climbing the four storeys to its 84ft high 'deck'. Halfway along its span, this footbridge offers a 360-degree view of London as never seen before.

SOUTH

Britannia Village, a thriving mix of local council, private, charity and housing association homes on the dock's south bank to the right, was established in 1994. Of the huge cranes that line the bank, fronting the warehouse-like housing estate, only two at the west end are originals. The curved housing block at the end of the bridge, with shops at ground level either side of its entrance, is a Peabody Trust development. Adjacent, to the left, is the curved glass roof of a separate private block that sits close to the as yet undeveloped stretch of land known as East Silvertown Quay. A vast, whitish 12-storey derelict 1930s block identified by red lettering spelling out the words 'Spillers' and 'Millennium Mills' dominates this side of the dock to the east. It is a legacy of the pontoon dock established 100 years ago for millers to offload, store and mill grain. Companies like Rank, the Co-op and Hovis once employed hundreds of people here; today, almost nothing remains except the cracked and empty Spillers building, an abandoned smaller brown brick warehouse complex next to it and a section of the Grade II listed Silo D peeping round beside the Peabody building.

Below at water level in dry dock sits the black and red steamer SS Robin, one of only three steamships in London to be classified with the nautical equivalent of a Grade I listing. Opposite, on the north side of Victoria Dock and taking up half its length is the ExCeL convention centre, with its iconic rooftop of white pipes in triangles. At the heart of London Docklands Development Corporation's regeneration of the Royals and intended as east London's answer to Earls Court and Olympia, ExCeL has virtually doubled in size since its original construction. With an extension completed in April 2010, it now provides a total of 100 million square feet of exhibition space. It will be a mainstay of the 2012 Olympic Games.

EAST

Across the eastern end, marked by a new pontoon bridge across its width, the road traffic never ceases across the Connaught Bridge behind it. The Connaught Bridge separates the Royal Victoria Dock from the other two Royals – the Royal George V on the south and the Royal Prince Albert on the north. To the right, the water of the George V Dock runs between the City Airport's brightly lit single island runway and the recently extended tarmacked airfield constructed on concrete piles.

Facing west, the low-rise angular Crystal at the dock entrance and white cable car terminus over the water beside it are dwarfed by the O₂ antennae to the left and Canary Wharf towers behind.

With the SS Robin *dry-docked in the foreground an airliner descends over Connaught Bridge to City Airport's runway beside the Albert Dock's water.*

more faintly silhouetted and form the horizon line, obscuring any view further west.

NORTHWEST

Beyond the water of the Royal Victoria Dock, the Olympic Park's red Orbit sculpture is spotted before the stadium itself, which is lower and lies alongside. Close by, the regenerated Royal Victoria development includes a fine new park next to ExCeL; *Landed*, a modern sculpture at its east end depicting four kinds of typical dockworkers, is visible from here. Westwards, next to the park, two hotels overlook the water facing Britannia Village. One large residential block with shops and restaurants on the promenade level anchors the rest of the north side.

From up here there is a splendid view of the west end of the dock where the tidal basin once was. It is currently undergoing complete reconstruction with two equally exciting projects. Not only is the Royal Victoria Dock the northern terminus of the Emirates Air Line cable car, but German engineering giant Siemens AG is currently building the two crystal glass structures of its Urban Sustainability Centre called The Crystal. The Royal Victoria will have been transformed again by the end of 2012.

Parallel to the runway, across to the north side, the length of water we see is the 2,000m long course of London's Regatta Centre. Along the quayside is Building 1000, one of Newham Borough's largest offices, and further east in the distance we can spot the 'D'-shaped faculty called the Knowledge Dock, built in 2000, that is part of the University of East London.

WEST

Turning 180 degrees, from this new vantage point the spikes of the O_2 Arena criss-cross the cranes on the dock's southern bank. In the near distance are the towers of Canary Wharf beyond rows of new residential developments along the Thames Pathway, which runs from the regenerated area of East India, on the Thames' north bank, to Blackwall. Beyond Canary Wharf, the City's newest landmark towers are

The Royal Victoria Dock Bridge

TRINITY BUOY WHARF LIGHTHOUSE

AN INTIMATE INSIGHT INTO A ONCE THRIVING INDUSTRIAL AREA

The name Trinity Buoy comes from the ancient Corporation of Trinity House, set up in Henry VIII's time and originally a voluntary association of shipmen and mariners granted a charter to erect and maintain beacons, marks and signs of the sea for safety and better navigation on the coasts of England. In 1803 this piece of land lent itself to creating a wharf originally used for storage of the buoys and chains bought in from outside manufacturers. The Corporation is still responsible for the country's buoys, lighthouses and light ships, even though they are no longer made or tested here. The lighthouse adjoins a building on the wharf called the Chain and Buoy Store.

Address 64 Orchard Place, E14 0JY
Nearest Tube East-India DLR
Open to the public? While the wharf is open to the public, the lighthouse has restricted entry times, especially at weekends
Disabled accessibility Yes
Website www.trinitybuoywharf.com
Contact details 020 7515 7153

The view from the last surviving lighthouse on London's Thames gives an unusually intimate insight into a once thriving industrial area that remained remote and virtually inaccessible, except from the river itself, for almost 200 years. One of East London's most unusual historic buildings, It was constructed in 1864 as part of a scientific workshop for the renowned 'father of electricity', Michael Faraday, who from the 1850s based his laboratories on this small peninsula of land where the Thames meets the mouth of Bow Creek.

The lighthouse's brick-lined spiral staircase rises to the first floor beneath the roof eaves, once the location of Faraday's research workshop and now an exhibiton space. From the narrow circular glazed space above, Faraday conducted tests of the experimental gas lamp that was eventually used in lighthouses and lightships around the country.

This cylindrical glass space at a gentle height of less than 100ft overlooks the Thames to the south. Initially the yellow spikes protruding from the domed roof of the O_2 Arena, on the Greenwich peninsula opposite,

Across Bow Creek from the red lightships HMS Warrior *was built in 1860.*

dominate the sightline. But the O_2 can't hide the sight of Shooters Hill beyond, even on a grey wet day. Today Faraday would have problems trying to use this hill to test his lamp thanks to a mass of transmission masts – ironically one of his legacies – being planted on top. Nor would he have been able to experience from up here as we can today the drama of one of the Thames' most vicious bends as it swirls round the Greenwich Peninsula. Steam and smoke belching from factories that lined both banks above would have obscured not only the myriad vessels waiting to moor or enter the docks upstream but the very geography that made the Port of London the world's busiest in the 19th century.

Adjacent to the eastern side of the O_2, we see a new cluster of green-blue glass office buildings. Just beside them an intriguing Antony Gormley sculpture, *Quantum Cloud* (yet another installation to celebrate the millennium), rises on its pontoon plinth from the Thames. The window at the top of the lighthouse is at just the right height from which to decipher the huge silhouetted male form composed of metal spikes that hovers in a cloud of metal shards.

EAST

The Leamouth is the point where Bow Creek (called the River Lea until it reaches Stratford about four miles to the north) and the Thames meet on a bend. The strong tidal influence on both these rivers has had a dramatic impact on the landscape, clearly visible from above as the tide ebbs. The grass-edged banks of Bow Creek near the river mouth take on a strange, desolate aspect as low tide reveals a deep riverbed, virtually devoid of water except for some greasy-looking trails through the black slimy sludge.

Still facing east from the lighthouse on the Trinity Buoy Wharf side of the Leamouth we look across to the masts of two Trinity House lightships. The lightships' engines have been removed but their cheerful red-painted surfaces lend a friendly maritime air to the view. Just a small leap across Bow Creek is a stretch of weed-covered tarmac with a few sheds. Not even a shadow remains of the once illustrious Thames Iron Works and Shipbuilding Company, established on that land from 1855. It is hard to believe that in 1861 Mechanics' Magazine described its premises as 'Leviathan Workshops ... of a truly Cyclopean type'. It was

West, past the moored Thames Clippers, towards Canary Wharf.

here that the buoys and chains for Trinity House Corporation were also manufactured, but the shipbuilder's lasting claim to fame is as the birthplace of the largest warship ever to be built in its day: the 9000-ton frigate HMS *Warrior*, launched in 1860.

WEST

Look now to the opposite side from the lighthouse and see the magnificent curve of the Thames as it stretches westward away from Trinity Buoy Wharf and its bright yellow converted container offices. On the north bank the new clusters of tall offices and residences that have sprung up in the last ten years look like a satellite overspill from Canary Wharf – although at East India they encircle the old East India Dock, as opposed to the West India Dock. Along the Virginia Quay that separates East India from Trinity Buoy Wharf and its lighthouse there is an unbroken line of new medium-height residences built in old-style yellow London stock brick. Their terraces and balconies overlook a public promenade that has replaced the noisy myriad of wharves, warehouses and factories that served the old docks. The Trinity Buoy Lighthouse lamp may be defunct but from up here at night a new light shines: a green laser beam cast upwards into the sky marks the zero meridian.

BECKTON ALP

A GRITTY AND UNIQUE URBAN LOCATION FROM WHICH TO VIEW LONDON'S ROMANTIC SKYLINE

Driving east along the A13 Tilbury Road, a grass-covered mound appears on the right by the East Ham turnoff. Not a natural hill, this is a slagheap created by the industrial residues of gas making at the Gas Light and Coke Company of Beckton. Having closed in 1969, it was transformed into Beckton Alp, being covered with an artificial snow surface to become London's first outdoor ski slope. Unlike the successful regeneration of Beckton itself, where thousands of new homes were built in the 1980s, the attraction failed. Today it stands like a freak hill on Alpine Way with the Beckton Retail Park and Alpine Retail Centre beside it.

Address Southeast of the junction of Newham Way and Woolwich Manor Way, E6
Nearest Tube Beckton DLR
Disabled accessibility Steep slope

Not recommended for a quiet family picnic, the top of Beckton Alp nevertheless offers a uniquely gritty, even 'skanky', urban location from which to view London's romantic skyline. Don't be deterred by the unsightly path to the summit. Perseverance will be rewarded by an unobscured 360-degree view of the metropolis, enabling appraisal of the dovetailing of Docklands regeneration into that brought about by the Olympic project. With the London Borough of Newham busy building on the advantage of hosting over half of the 2012 Games venues, this flattened hillcrest, just 115ft high, offers a unique viewpoint from which to reappraise metropolitan London's eastward shift.

WEST

On the western horizon, beyond the acres of red-brick terraced houses with pitched roofs of New Beckton below, the skyline picks out a revealing panorama of every new high-rise signature building in central London. Viewing from north to south (or right to left), the City towers, the Shard, Canary Wharf and the antennae of the O_2 Arena on the south bank line up. The O_2 itself is almost obscured by the high-rise residential and office towers of East India alongside the old East India Dock Basin on the Thames' north bank.

To the north, the A13 ramps up at Beckton to bypass East Ham and Barking. Traffic high above ground level rips across the foreground but vehicle noise is eerily muted. Across the highway the view consists of more acres of homes, playing fields, cemeteries and schools in East Ham, Plaistow and Manor Park. None of these areas were even part of London until the 1960s. This was Essex.

Just a handful of high-rise blocks, including Newham's largest sixth-form college, stand out. The grand square red-brick clock tower of Newham Town Hall and to the west the Boleyn Ground, West Ham United's football stadium, break up the urban sprawl that stretches north as far as the neighbouring borough of Redbridge. Slightly to the west the new high-rise residential towers

West from Beckton Alp up the A13, with the City in the distance.

of Stratford High Street frame the southern edge of the Olympic Park, where the viewing platform level of Anish Kapoor's Orbit sculpture takes shape just behind. On a clear day, the hill on the horizon where Alexandra Palace stands in Haringey is just visible about 15 miles away diagonally across central London.

Behind the black glass and white concrete façade of Newham University Hospital's new Gateway Surgical Centre, the main road curves southwest to Canning Town, currently undergoing a complete £3.7 billion rebuild. Just beyond stands the unmistakable silhouette of controversial architect Erno Goldfinger's Balfron Tower in Poplar, with its linked tower that houses the building's communal utilities.

The former ski slope at Beckton Alp with the Beckton Retail Park beyond.

SOUTH

Turning towards the south, two tall smoking chimney towers belong to Newham's vast and historic sugar refining complex, once owned by Tate and Lyle but sold off in 2010 to American Sugar Refiners to Newham's consternation.

In the middle distance on the north bank of the Thames are the waters of the Albert Dock, with Building 1000, home to Newham Council's offices, close to the junction of the Albert and Victoria Docks. Along the dockside stands the University of East London's Knowledge Dock, its neighbouring new drum-shaped residence halls with sloping roofs just discernible. Between that line and where we stand the view is dominated by the roofs of the Alpine Business Centre in the foreground.

London City Airport on the George V dockside, parallel to Albert Dock, is not clearly visible from here but the planes descending and ascending every few minutes testify to the presence of its runway that divides the two docks.

EAST

Turning towards the east, more university halls and sports facilities are under construction and the bright orange, red and yellow wall of Gallions Reach Station comes into view where an abandoned Thames Gateway project leaves a bridge going nowhere. Beyond the industrial landscape around Beckton Sewage Treatment Works is the tall 'H' shaped Barking Creek Flood Barrier. This is where the River Roding – once the boundary between Greater London and Essex – flows southwards into the Thames.

Turning again to face northeast, we see the point on the skyline where London comes to an end, giving way to the countryside landscape of Essex on the horizon. And we have come full circle. In this direction a few brand new brightly coloured high-rise towers surround the elegant clock tower and domed cupola of Barking and Dagenham Town Hall. Built in the 1930s, this little-recorded landmark was where legendary singer-songwriter Neil Young recorded two live tracks for his *Harvest* album at a concert in 1972.

SHOOTERS HILL AND ANKERDINE CRESCENT

A COMPREHENSIVE VIEW OF LONDON FROM A HISTORICALLY IMPORTANT LOOKOUT

Shooters Hill was once on the principal route from London to Dover and thereby to the continent. Its highest point is 432ft above sea level, giving a comprehensive view of London looking northwest. There is a fine heath – also called Shooters Hill – to the west, Somewhat like a south London equivalent of Hampstead Heath, it links open meadows and woodlands like Oxleas Wood, Jack Wood, Castle Wood and Eltham Common. And like Hampstead Heath, it has played an important role in London's ancient and modern history. Both have served as strategic lookout points over London – most recently during the Second World War. Shooters Hill suffered for it, becoming the Luftwaffe's bomb dumping ground. Any live bombs that remained on board German warplanes returning across the Channel from London bombing sorties would be released as a precaution before the planes headed back to home territory.

Address Ankerdine Crescent, SE18
Nearest Tube Woolwich Arsenal DLR
Open To The Public? Yes
Disabled accessibility Steep hill

ANKERDINE CRESCENT

Down a small parallel steep street east of Shooters Hill called Ankerdine Crescent is an unusual narrow vista down to the Thames where it rounds the Greenwich Peninsula. The O₂ Arena's roof with its yellow antennae stands out beside the host of new facilities surrounding it. This little stretch of riverside at North Charlton remains highly industrial, laden with piles of aggregates, concrete mixing facilities and conveyor belts.

Across the river from here are the low roofs of the homes of Britannia Village on the south side of Victoria Dock and the tall new apartments of the north, while a glimpse of a forked tower offers the first evidence of London's newest connection over the Thames, the Emirates Air Line cable car linking the Greenwich peninsula with the ExCeL and Royal Victoria Dock. This view indicates exactly where the crossing is located. From Ankerdine Crescent the distance between the Dock and the Olympic Park is compressed to make it look as if the Olympic Stadium itself is standing right

The powerhouse skyline of the City seen from a leafy south London hilltop.

behind the Victoria Dock towers, with the red tubing of its Orbit neighbour sticking out at a two o'clock angle.

Look a little further east and the shining piers of the Thames Barrier march across the river between Woolwich on the southern side and Silvertown's Thames Barrier Park on the north bank. There, the Barrier Point housing complex looks like a huge white cruise liner run aground on the park's western edge. Its single round white tower like a ship's funnel stands right on the banks of the river, while behind it the rest of the ship splays out with its broad white decks stepping down to the lawns.

SHOOTERS HILL

Away from Ankerdine Crescent, the best point from which to absorb the all-encompassing London skyline at Shooters Hill would theoretically be from the top of Severndroog Castle in Castle Wood. The castle, a memorial built by a certain Lady James to her husband Sir William in 1785, is in a sadly dilapidated state. It has been closed off to the public although funds appear to be available for its restoration. Like most of Shooters Hill at its highest points, the surrounding land is too heavily wooded to give a good view. The answer is to stand at the summit on a traffic island on Shooters Hill Road, although this is not recommended at busy times of day!

From here London lies deep in a valley surrounded by the hills of Harrow and Essex some 20 miles to the north and east. The hill is so steep here that almost nothing at the bottom around Kidbrooke and Blackheath can be seen. South London only becomes visible with the new mixed high- and low-rise Woolwich and Charlton housing estates by the Thames. Very little else can be distinguished apart from the landmark towers of Greenwich Power Station on the bank of the Thames, with the Shard going up behind it, and the low-lying 11-acre Harmsworth Printing works at Surrey Quays.

The distance between here and central London is roughly ten miles, so strange combinations of buildings stack up together like Tower Bridge with the BT Tower right behind it and the arch of Wembley Stadium just behind that. The raking light on a bright but cloudy day throws into sharp relief random features of this view, such as the cross-bracing all the way down the glass façade of the Broadgate Tower on the Bishopsgate side of the City and the white spokes of the London Eye.

A glimpse of the O₂ and Royal Docks looking northeast from Shooters Hill towards Silvertown.

GREENWICH PARK

LONDON'S MOST IMPRESSIVE THAMESSIDE VIEW, ENJOYED FOR CENTURIES BY ROMANS, SAXONS AND NORMANS

The riverside at Greenwich became a royal home when Henry V's younger brother built a palace called Bella Court in 1427. For the next two hundred years, much of Greenwich was a favourite royal hunting ground. The Royal Armouries of Henry VIII (no longer in existence) and the Royal Observatory built by Charles II have always assured Greenwich of a prominent place in English history. Archaeological finds in the park have confirmed that this view must have been enjoyed for centuries by Romans, Saxons and Normans. UNESCO calls this Heritage Site a 'remarkably intact historic landscape'.

Address Charlton Way
Nearest Tube Cutty Sark DLR
Open To The Public? 6am-8pm
Disabled accessibility Yes
Website www.royalparks.org.uk
Contact details 0300 061 2000

A visit to Greenwich today usually includes a steep climb to see the house and observatory of Astronomer Royal John Flamsteed, purpose-built overlooking the park by Sir Christopher Wren in 1675. Visitors reaching the top of the hill find it impossible not to be distracted by London's most impressive Thamesside view from beneath the bronze statue of General Wolfe of Quebec.

NORTHWEST

The huge expanse of Greenwich Park keeps the palatial developments below at a respectful distance from the viewer. The striking layout of this group of elegant 17th-to 20th-century whiteish stone and painted buildings is a sight of pleasing symmetry. The first building before us, and the oldest we see, is the snow-white Queen's House, built for Queen Anne, Danish wife of James I. Designed by architect Inigo Jones, it was the first Palladian-style classical house to be built in England, although its elegant colonnaded wings were added only in the first decade of the 19th century.

Several leading late 17th-century architects had a hand in the symmetry of Greenwich Palace as we see it today. But all had to respect that the view from Queen's House to the river was sacrosanct. William and Mary's decision to turn the project into a home for retired and invalided seamen known as the Old Royal Naval College meant the new palace, built in four main blocks, was never a royal home. The King William and Queen Mary blocks (those with the pepperpot cupolas on the top) are open in part to the public, the rest belonging to the University of Greenwich. The two blocks beyond these, set wider apart by the riverside, are named King Charles and Queen Anne and today are occupied by the Trinity Laban Conservatoire of Music and Dance and the University of Greenwich respectively.

Anyone who has studied maps of London will instantly recognise the dramatic sweep of the Thames as it swirls around the tongue of land we call the Isle of Dogs. Beyond the stern baroque of the palace on the south bank, we see between the King Charles and Queen Anne blocks a stretch of the Thames and, sitting on the tip of the Isle of Dogs, the north side's Island Gardens, from which vantage point Canaletto painted the view where we stand on the hill.

The buildings that have grown up to left and right of the Isle of Dogs riverside are largely the legacy of the London Docklands Development Corporation. Along the water's edge

The Queen's House and the Royal Naval College at Greenwich with a fabulous backdrop of high-rise London.

The panoramic view from the top of Greenwich Park sweeps all the way to St Paul's with Hampstead and Highgate Hills beyond.

The skyscrapers of Docklands soar up to dwarf Inigo Jones's Queen's House.

they gradually increase in height until they are topped off at the northernmost end of the peninsula by the new skyline icons of Canary Wharf, the most outstanding always the blinking pyramid-topped tower of Number One Canada Square. Canary Wharf's towers obscure the view due north, but as we look to the left and right London flares out on either side.

WEST

To the far west there is an unusual view of the south side of the river opposite the Isle of Dogs. On the regenerated Surrey Quays from Canada Water northwards is the giant expanse of the Harmsworth Printing facility, meeting the last of the remaining Convoys Wharf on the Lewisham riverside where once the paper industry was served with imports. This old freight wharf has a preservation order on it – unlike most of the Rotherhithe peninsula

which from here is clearly outlined, its seamless line of rebuilt homes tracing the curve of the river's edge.

Behind, and beyond the bend in the river going west, is the City with its new glass towers, clustered together except for the Broadgate Tower (easily recognised by its cross-bracing). Looking across to the City from this angle it stands somewhat isolated from its contemporaries although it is barely more than a quarter of a mile away. The majestic dome of St Paul's leads the eye northwest to the twin hills of Hampstead and Highgate on the horizon. The length rather than the sheer density of this view gives a thrill.

NORTH

With your back now facing the black wrought-iron Observatory gates, all the major London venues of the 2012 Games make an appearance. The equestrian events will take place in Greenwich Park itself and to the right of Canary Wharf's towers we have a splendid view in the distance of the Olympic Stadium's white spikey mesh of light towers. From this angle, to the north of Greenwich Power Station's brick chimneys is an 'echo' view of the O_2 Arena's spikey yellow quadrapods. It will be known as North Greenwich Arena when it hosts the gymnastics and the finals of several other Olympic events. Beyond the O_2 and the opaque plastic 'grow tunnels' of David Beckham's now defunct Footballing Academy, on the north bank of the Thames the rooftop triangular white tubing of the ExCeL Centre comes into view on the far side of the Royal Victoria Dock. ExCeL will host 13 Olympic and Paralympic sports. From here it is also possible to see the crystalline Siemens urban sustainability centre, known as The Crystal, under construction at the western end of the dock.

CERISE ROAD CAR PARK, PECKHAM RYE

ONE OF THE MOST SATISFYINGLY DIFFERENT VANTAGE POINTS FOR SKYLINE VIEWING IN LONDON

An indoor multi-storey car park off Rye Lane with an entrance to the Peckham Plex cinema on the ground floor may not sound promising for skyline views – especially as its roof is closed off. But climb up to the highest of its publicly accessible levels, level 5, and by way of a series of pane-less concrete bunker-type windows it becomes one of the most satisfyingly different vantage points for skyline viewing in London. In recent years a 'pop-up' venue called Frank's Café and Campari Bar, thriving under a temporary canopy, has presented art exhibitions alongside drinks and dining on the roof level in the summer months.

Address Cerise Road, SE15 5HQ
Nearest Tube Peckham Rye National Rail
Open To The Public? Yes
Disabled accessibility No

The series of oblong, deeply recessed window apertures on the fifth floor of Cerise Road Car Park give the view an unusually focused feel. Sometimes a lower line of vision can reveal a more complex narrative to a familiar skyline theme. Viewing the skyline from the roof would give no added benefit. It would simply be a different experience.

Looking due north it is as if these window openings divide central London into three sections. The middle distance with its famous silhouettes becomes the subject for a series of framed 'paintings', apparently arranged for viewing convenience on a high east–west plateau. The view rises up from the lower-lying plane of Peckham, Camberwell, Bermondsey and Rotherhithe south of the Thames, the local scenery in the foreground from each window creating the setting for the high drama in the middle distance. The far distance, taking up at least half of each frame, is simply sky. The fifth-floor perspective is like that when sitting on the ground looking up to watch the action above and beyond as, for example, at a children's glove puppet show.

Peckham Rye is in the foreground of this linear series of recessed windows. Many new angular and rounded rooftops are prominent features around old Peckham Square. They stem from recent initiatives in the

A foreground curtain of local flats on a low line of vision frames the rising towers of Canary Wharf behind.

public realm – the pedestrianisation of busy shopping streets, the new Peckham Pulse fitness centre and the emerging Copeland Cultural Quarter adjacent to Peckham Rye Station – interspersed among the perpendicular rows of mainly Victorian terraced rooftops and chimneystacks.

NORTH

From the middle of the three windows, the south-facing front elevation of Peckham's eye-catching library, shaped like an upside-down 'L', splashes a welcome stripe of turquoise onto the 'canvas'. Next to the word 'LIBRARY' in white lettering fixed to the roofline sit a pair of conical lead-covered domes like grey bosoms on the roof either side of an elevated burnt-orange oval plate structure. That turns out to be the top of the central glass atrium inside the building. Its ellipsoidal shape protrudes above and beyond the flat rooftop line and suddenly the Shard, looking like some kind of transmission tower, pokes upwards from directly

behind the library with the tower of Guy's Hospital beside. Turning very slightly westward, the library's roof provides an exciting foil to the more conventional dome and pepperpot-topped west towers of St Paul's sitting neatly in the middle distance about four miles away.

Immediately behind the right-hand corner of Peckham's library roof, the familiar cone top of City Hall and the south tower of Tower Bridge with its golden finials are decipherable among the steel and glass blocks lining the south bank of the Thames. Rising up on a hill on the river's north bank, the City of London landmarks range themselves from left to right: the Gherkin, Tower 42, the scooped-fronted black glass Willis Building. And just to the right is the standalone green glass rectangle of Broadgate Tower, north of Bishopsgate.

NORTHWEST

The view to the west of Peckham's library from the left-hand window

is framed in the foreground by the barrel glass atrium roof covering the shops of the Aylesham Centre, and by the white stone clock tower with weathervane of the old Jones and Higgins store on the north side of Peckham Square and the rooftops of the old school house of St James the Great Primary School. Beyond those, to the north in the middle distance stands a row of central London signatures including the London Eye, the Shell Tower, the Shard, the BT Tower and Centre Point. The pretty 210ft high white stone tower of St Giles, Camberwell marks the extreme west limitation from the car park's fifth-floor window.

NORTHEAST

The three residential towers much closer to this car park viewpoint belong to Avondale Square Estate, about a mile due north from here between the Old Kent Road and

Will Alsop's green Peckham Library steals the show from the Shard in this view. Guy's Hospital Tower is to its left.

Rolls Road. To their right sits the gas holder of the Southeastern Gasworks off the Old Kent Road. Looking diagonally northeast past it, the renovated brick and concrete high-rise tower blocks of South Bermondsey and the Rotherhithe housing estates on the filled-in Surrey Docks spread out towards the top of the peninsula.

Diagonally across the Thames, only the green-topped Four Seasons Hotel at the Westferry end of Canary Wharf identifies where the riverbank of the Isle of Dogs is located. From the extreme eastern window, the skyline presents Canary Wharf's banking and office towers as a crowd of sinister grey giants peering down at and dwarfing all other buildings around the old Millwall Docks below them.

THE POINT AT POINT HILL

AN INTIMATE SIGHT OF GREENWICH, NEIGHBOURING DEPTFORD AND BEYOND

The Point is a tiny public green on one level that could be mistaken for a private garden. High up and tucked away among the smart houses around the top of Greenwich Park and Blackheath, it opens long views of central London's breadth and depth from Battersea Water Tower at its western end to the Orbit sculpture at the Olympic Park in the east.

Address Point Hill, SE10
Nearest Tube Greenwich DLR

The point of The Point's view is its unusual site. Sitting as it does on a sheer escarpment, apart from the long views it also offers an intimate sight of rapidly regenerating historic Greenwich and neighbouring Deptford situated immediately below.

NORTH

The view from the east side of The Point, partially obscured by trees, locates the viewer in the heart of Greenwich, which is easily identified by the orange brick clock tower of the old 1930s town hall. It is juxtaposed with the pretty white stone tower of Greenwich's parish church, St Alphege – designed by Nicholas Hawksmoor in the 18th century – just visible through the trees. The dramatic foreground drop does not obscure the lines of quality houses whose architectural design varies between late 18th-and early 19th-century styles. These have been joined by contemporary blocks of flats and civic amenities quite consistent and complementary with their older neighbours in colour and materials.

On the east side of Deptford Creek a row of new six-storey yellow and white façade blocks of flats with balconies, Tarves Way, dominates the local Greenwich view. In front of these the bright red Docklands Light Railway trains snake every few minutes along the high level tracks through Greenwich Station – a classic 1830s two-storey brick and stone coursework building and one of the oldest surviving original railway stations in the country. It stands right beside the new brick Novotel hotel with its two top storeys in bright green. The original terminus of that railway track, the first ever built in this country, running across meadowland, on a viaduct from

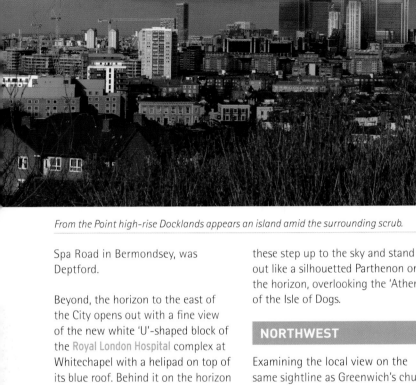

From the Point high-rise Docklands appears an island amid the surrounding scrub.

Spa Road in Bermondsey, was Deptford.

Beyond, the horizon to the east of the City opens out with a fine view of the new white 'U'-shaped block of the Royal London Hospital complex at Whitechapel with a helipad on top of its blue roof. Behind it on the horizon hill, to the right, Alexandra Palace is clearly silhouetted in the distance, some 15 miles away.

Closer in, on the banks of the Isle of Dogs opposite, the regenerated riverside housing fronts the taller office blocks at the South Dock of Canary Wharf. The Point offers an unusual angle on Canary Wharf: for once the bunch of giant glass towers to the east are upstaged by the lower pale cream and beige stone of the Chicago-style buildings around the eastern, Cabot Square, end. From here

these step up to the sky and stand out like a silhouetted Parthenon on the horizon, overlooking the 'Athens' of the Isle of Dogs.

NORTHWEST

Examining the local view on the same sightline as Greenwich's church of St Alphege but further west, the fine clock tower and pediment of St Paul's Church, the parish church of neighbouring Deptford, reveals itself above the trees of its surrounding park. Coincidentally, by looking in a straight line behind the Deptford St Paul's some four miles away across the Thames, the dome and lantern of Sir Christopher Wren's cathedral in the City suddenly appears.

Wren would have been gratified to see how his St Paul's achieves splendid isolation from here, with sky above and the gentle slope of Highgate Hill behind. In the 21st century the whole of the City stands out to perfection from The Point's modest height, with the towering steel and glass neighbours of St Paul's silhouetted against the sky to its right and the glossy Shard and matt-coated Guy's Hospital Tower to the left.

The Thames itself is minimally visible from the Point; we can only catch glimpses here and there between new housing developments on the south side of the river. Even the massive Millennium Quays development that replaced the old riverside Deptford Power Station just 12 years ago has been obscured by even newer clusters of apartment and office blocks further inland.

The backs of those four new turquoise glass pavilions of varying height, known as Creekside Village West, front onto the ancient Creek Road that crosses Deptford Creek to Greenwich. But from here Creekside provides the backdrop to the award-winning silver-roofed Laban Centre for Music and Dance, abutting Deptford Creek on the west side. It stands in its own landscaped gardens, its pastel-coloured translucent walls curved to catch the light and attention. Finished in 2003, the Centre has turned 'inland' Deptford's fortunes around and linked it to the more dynamic changes already seen on its riverside.

The Point's modest height achieves a perfectly comprehensive view of the City and Westminster.

TELEGRAPH HILL PARK

A FRESH ANGLE ON LONDON'S MOST RENOWNED LANDMARKS

The telegraph in the name of this park in New Cross, Lewisham refers to a semaphore station established here in 1795 by the Admiralty, connecting London to Deal, Dover and the Continent. Telegraph Hill was instrumental in transmitting news of Wellington's victory at Waterloo. Previously the hill had been known as Garlick Plow Hill. In what was then a heavily wooded part of Surrey, it would have had a direct view across the Thames to the roof of the Admiralty in Whitehall that was completed by the 1720s. The view of Whitehall no longer exists and on the highest spot, where the station once stood, there are tennis courts today.

Address Kitto Road, SE14
Nearest Tube Nunhead National Rail

 Telegraph Hill stands among endless streets of three- and four-storey terraced houses climbing neighbouring hills. At just 125ft above sea level, the Hill still offers a view of the entire canon of London's skyline signature buildings, although at its best when the trees are not in leaf.

Looking down at the London of the near distance, it feels that planned development of the capital's southern suburbs in the late 19th century was much more successful and less random than that of their north London equivalents. From here the shopping streets, town halls, parks and transport systems make this side of the Thames feel far more complete in itself and less dependent on central London. Indeed, less than five miles away the City and Westminster look strangely remote.

NORTH

Due north down to New Cross Gate, we overlook one of the country's oldest routes to Westminster. The line of the Old Kent Road trails off to the west through Peckham past the barrel-shaped glass atriums of the Aylesham Centre through Bermondsey, to a London Bridge not visible but indelibly marked by the Shard. This was the route Chaucer's pilgrims took to Canterbury in the 14th century, who would have had a stunning view to the Thames through the surrounding woods. Today there is no sight of the river.

Tucked into the middle distance to the east, the chimney of Tate Modern pokes its way skyward above its top two pale green glass storeys. From this angle, St Paul's Cathedral for once does not figure in the view. Instead, Tate Modern would appear to be directly opposite Fleet Street and the curved roofs of Peterborough Court and the spire of St Bride's Church.

NORTHWEST

Other famous landmarks' locations can seem slightly distorted from this angle. The tops of the Victoria and Big Ben towers of the Palace of Westminster look oddly estranged – miles from each other. Trees close by obscuring full view make the landmarks miles away, such as the Hilton on Park Lane and Euston Tower, fill the apparently big gap between them. Once home of Capital Radio,

today the latter houses HM Revenue and Customs. From this angle on west London, the circular top floors of the BT Tower appear to be placed on the roof of Centre Point.

Apart from the Shard, the most prominent building is the Strata on Walworth Road, appearing pencil slim. With its half-turned 'back' to us, the rear façade is clearly concave and the forward slope of its roof is much steeper than seen from the north. The London Eye looks attached to its right side – like some huge rotating mechanism by which the black and white tower is wound up. Unusually, further west only two of Battersea Power Station's four white towers are visible, the two that frame the length of the building, not the two on the riverbank.

Two of Battersea Power Station's white chimneys are visible in the centre of the view.

THE SHARD

A GLASS PYRAMID IN THE SKY

Visible from all over the Capital and its outer suburbs, the 1017ft-high jagged-topped splinter of steel-framed glass called the Shard, designed by Renzo Piano, is the new spectre stalking London. Across London Bridge on the south bank of the Thames the Shard is destined to become a unique 72-storey luxury lifestyle oasis. Layers of offices, restaurants, a hotel, residences, a three-floor observatory, and conference rooms – in that order, bottom to top, will divide the building. With the city's skyline no longer dominated by church spires, the Shard will be the first pyramid – albeit an elongated one – to appear as a landmark on London's horizon. Due for completion in June 2012 but not open to the public until 2013, it will make London home to Europe's tallest building.

Address 32 London Bridge Street, SE1
Nearest Tube London Bridge
Open To The Public? **Not until 2013**
Disabled accessibility Yes
Website www.the-shard.com

Doubtless, the Shard's primacy will be brief, thanks to European capitals' 'tower one-upmanship': new taller structures are already said to be on the drawing board. But in Spring 2013 the luxury 200-bedroom Shangri-la Hotel opens, occupying 18 floors of the building. On floor 52, its highest level, , guests will be treated to joyful, heart-pounding 360-degree views, just as the architect intended, from its dining room, bar, gym and pool. In the same year, about three of the Shard's highest floors are expected to open to the public as a viewing gallery for a panorama of sensational views - the highest ever of the capital.

NORTH

The shapely giants of the City sitting opposite on the north bank have met their match. High-rise Southwark is on the map. As the first skyscraper in that location, the Shard windows offer a fresh take on London's skyline from every floor and direction. The view northwards reveals that the high and still-rising core of the Walkie Talkie (20 Fenchurch Street) is about to obscure the Heron Tower close behind. As the Shard's shape sharply pinches in towards its summit, across the Thames, in complete reverse, the Walkie Talkie silhouette will splay outwards as it rises upwards.

Just over halfway up the Shard's height, at roughly helicopter flight height, due north of the City, north London stretches out in relief against the sky. Even on a grey

Northwards towards the City and Essex beyond.

day all the way northeast the hills of Essex beyond Waltham Abbey and in the northwest the hills of Hertfordshire beyond Enfield and the M25 are now plainly visible from the South bank!

Facing north to northeast in the middle distance the view clearly shows how London is moving east. The building work around Stratford and the Olympic Park and to its south, now clearly links up a myriad of routes into the City from up here. Between the Thames below and the Olympic Park stadium one prominent landmark building is the bulky blue new Royal London Hospital whose rooftop helipad can only just be distinguished at this height. Coincidentally, the same firm of architects – Populous – formerly known as HOK, designed the hospital and the landmark Olympic Stadium.

EAST

Piano's Shard is breaking the South-wark mould. In traditional real estate thinking, building luxurious high-profile accommodation adjacent to London's busy railway hub, London Bridge Station, would be foolhardy. But from up here looking eastwards the massive span of parallel railway tracks into London Bridge Station immediately below is a more mesmer-ising view than the flow of the mighty Thames. The white and green trains snaking out from both east and west sides of the Shard eclipse the river's activity unfolding close by. Trailing out eastwards on the viaducts that raise the trains to the height of the surrounding buildings, the history of London's transport narrative unfolds before our eyes in utter silence.

The higher the window view from the Shard the more the Thames is reduced to a meandering stream. It flows under London Bridge with the Tower of London laid out beside it like a Legoland pastiche on the north bank and City Hall looking like a lop-sided sugar bowl with lid on the south.

SOUTH

To the south for once the striped Strata and its roof turbines appear surprisingly close enough for scrutiny. They are whizzing round! Has the wind changed? Have the engineers solved the noise problem that some say is the reason these turbines ceased turning? Until the arrival of the Shard, this residential tower was a solitary south London landmark in the generally low-rise south London context.

Bang up against the south-facing windows is the Shard's little old uncle: the 1970s grey concrete Guy's Tower which until now was London Bridge south side's highest skyline landmark. Just to the west of it and directly below we overlook the original palatial-style layout of Guy's Hospital situated around a rectangular main courtyard with twin courtyards to its rear. Philanthropic bookseller Thomas Guy built it in the early 18th century, with the proceeds of his successful South Sea investments, as an annex to the ancient St Thomas' Hospital.

WEST

The magnificent dropdown view over riverside south London to the West from the Shard's sloping windows is

The swerving course of the Thames is superbly visible.

pure revelation. Pockets of Southwark appear marshalled into densely built-up 'islands' by the swirl of railway tracks. It is a vision of jaw-dropping drama, aided by the bright red cranes like magic wands hovering over new sites rising from the ground at London Bridge Quarter – the name now for the old London Bridge Station terminus area that remains above ground level to meet the viaduct tracks. Next to Borough High Street and hemmed in by London Bridge and Borough Market's new white handkerchief roof, Southwark Cathedral's blond stone tower with its four spiky finials looks feisty enough to see off the threat of any developers.

The red-brick Wren-style tower with distinctive white cornerstones of St Thomas the Apostle church, built in 1703, stands out on St Thomas Street below. It is a reminder that an earlier medieval church on the site gave its name to the ancient Southwark hospital today relocated in Lambeth. This church and the hospital were originally named for St Thomas Beckett, the saint in the sights of Chaucer's pilgrims who set off from here to Canterbury in the late 14th-century.

Upstream the Thames wends its way under the Millennium Bridge, which is almost too fine to distinguish clearly from here on a cloudy day. Its location can only be ascertained by spotting the modest (from this height) brick chimney of Tate Modern.

A river of railway lines flowing out of London Bridge Station.

Beyond, towards the southwest, the almost-finished circular pepper mill of a tower known as One St George's Wharf at Vauxhall Cross prefaces the four white towers of Battersea Power Station close by as the local landmark.

The sheer extent of this view is a stun factor hard to put into words. After rain, the sun-drenched Chiltern Hills on the horizon beyond Gerrards Cross and even Beaconsfield, are simply breathtaking. Between now and Spring 2013 we will have the chance to mentally compose ourselves for the prospect of even richer skyline vistas when the Shard will allow the general public access to its fizzy new viewing experience.

OXO TOWER BUILDING

A VIEW TARGETING THE POINT WHERE THE TWIN CITIES OF LONDON AND WESTMINSTER MEET

In 1929 the Liebig Extract of Meat Company, manufacturer of the Oxo cube, bought this reconstructed power station on the south bank of the Thames. Cleverly circumventing the laws forbidding large-scale advertising on the river, company architect Albert W. Moore installed in the tower's three vertical windows red-coloured panes shaped to read the word 'OXO'. The tower could be lit up and seen from afar, day or night. By the 1970s the company had moved away, and the building was threatened with demolition until it was saved by a successful local campaign in 1984. The refurbished building, reopened in 1996, has a bar, brasserie and restaurant on the top floor.

Address Bargehouse Street, SE1 9PH
Nearest Tube Blackfriars
Open To The Public? Restaurant and bar on top floor
Disabled accessibility Yes
Website www.coinstreet.org
Contact details 020 7021 1600

From the south bank of the Thames by the Pool of London the view from the Oxo Tower's brasserie targets the point where the twin cities of London and Westminster meet on the north bank. Many of the institutions we can see from here define not only London but England itself. Yet although most Londoners would recognise the buildings in these views, very few would be able to tell you what they are.

NORTH

HMS President, a retired 1918 sloop, is moored straight ahead off the Victoria Embankment, which runs along the north bank between the River Thames and two of the four Inns of Court where barristers have their chambers. The gardens fronting

the Embankment belong to the Middle Temple Inn to the left, which is divided from the Inner Temple Gardens on the right by Middle Temple Lane that runs from Fleet Street down to the Embankment. To the right of Inner Temple Gardens is a row of three conservation-listed houses in contrasting architectural styles. The red-brick Tudor-style Gothic mansion, Sion House, was built as a meeting place and library for Anglican clergy. Behind, the skyline of Fleet Street displays the five-tiered bell tower of St Bride's Church, believed to be the inspiration for the first tiered wedding cake.

NORTHEAST

Back on the Embankment, the building to the right of Sion House with an impressively steep roof is the grey stone French Renaissance-style villa that until 1968 housed the City of London Boys' School. Behind it is the domed roof of the Old Bailey – the highest criminal court in the land. The curved white stone baroque building with a screen of classical colonnades that snakes around the corner of the Embankment into Bridge Street is the 1930s headquarters of Unilever – the world's largest manufacturer of food and hygiene products. Beside it is the new Blackfriars Bridge with its over-the-river railway station.

To the right above the bridge is an excellent view of St Paul's on the top of Ludgate Hill. At street level it is not apparent that this is the steepest hill in the City, but from this angle, the bright green copper roof of Faraday House on Queen Victoria Street stands out because St Paul's behind it is so high up. To its right is a gap, before the refitted green glass Stock Exchange Tower imposes itself in front

The Embankment from the Oxo Tower. The Dome of the Old Bailey is just visible to the left of the curved white Unilever House.

of Tower 42 and the Heron Tower in the heart of the City.

NORTHWEST

Leaving the extreme right-hand side of the view, the gardens of the Middle Temple mark the point on the Victoria Embankment where the boundaries of Westminster and the ancient Square Mile meet. The boundary between the City and Westminster was for centuries the site where colliers on the Thames had to stop and pay tax on coal shipments destined for the City. Today a memorial stone arch on the pavement of the Victoria Embankment identifies that important location and two silver dragons on plinths either side of the road, each with crested shield and crimson tongue, mark where the City meets Westminster, but neither they nor the arch are visible from here. The mass of steep roofs, spires and towers on the skyline behind the Middle Temple Garden identify the Royal Courts of Justice on the Strand, in the borough of Westminster.

A white stone building in two symmetrical halves linked by a green copper arch stands out on Temple Place, to the west (left) of Middle Temple Gardens. Formerly Electra House, originally built for the Cable and Wireless Company which created the world's first global cable communications network, it was rebuilt as Globe House and is now the home of British American Tobacco. It is said that this building was home to the secret Foreign Office department that planned propaganda during the Second World War. Appropriately enough the BT Tower is visible in the far distance, while to the left on the skyline is Centre Point. Next to it is the white bulk of the Royal Opera House rooftop. From here the Opera House appears to stand on a hilltop directly above the riverside palace of Somerset House, recognisable by the green dome above its colonnaded riverside entrance.

SOUTHWEST

Just behind the four spans of Westminster Bridge over the river, the monumental Shell Mex House fills the skyline. This 1930s behemoth of a building, occupying the block from the Strand down to the Embankment, was purpose-built for the Shell Oil Company. Its clock tower – the largest in London, with dashes instead of numbers – helped make it a signature building in its day. To its right the skyline and riverside are dominated by Terry Farrell's Embankment Place, the 1980s office block built over Charing Cross station; on the other side of Northumberland Avenue where it meets Victoria Embankment is the light brown curve of London's newest luxury corner hotel, the Corinthia.

TATE MODERN

A UNIQUELY VEHICLE-FREE VIEW ACROSS THE THAMES TO ST PAUL'S

The chimney tower of decommissioned Bankside Power Station, an icon (or eyesore) of Southwark's skyline, seemed an unlikely symbol of regeneration 15 years ago. Yet the success of architects Herzog de Meuron's £134m conversion of this industrial structure into the world's most visited gallery of international modern art has led the way for a stream of culture-led regeneration projects throughout the country. With hindsight it is easy to see how the simultaneously constructed Millennium Bridge across the Thames, connecting Tate Modern to St Paul's Cathedral on the north bank, proved to be the making of Bankside on the south.

Address Bankside, SE1 9TG
Nearest Tube Southwark
Open To The Public? Sun-Thurs 10am-6pm, Fri-Sat 10am-10pm; No entry fee
Disabled accessibility Yes
Website www.tate.org.uk
Contact details 020 7887 8888

The view from Tate Modern's glass-fronted sixth- and seventh-floor extension largely ignores Bankside to celebrate the City of London, with St Paul's Cathedral taking centre stage. This view immediately seems static and peaceful. There is something very Canaletto-esque about it, because apart from one small ramp down to the Embankment this is a uniquely road-less, car-less view. Crowds fill the walkways on either side of the river and across the Millennium Bridge, while the only vehicle traffic is relatively silent, coming as it does from pleasure catamarans and clippers on the Thames.

On an early frosty blue-sky morning, as low sunlight streams through the cables of sculptor Anthony Caro's bridge, also known as the 'Blade of Light', and reflects off window panes to dance on the river, the 'professionals' keen to protect London's historically and culturally sensitive areas from development are vindicated. The pleasure of this view is lasting. That is undoubtedly the result of unflinching respect for the sightline of St Paul's from the riverside as well as from various vantage points in the surrounding City streets.

NORTH

Straight ahead on the river bank, adjacent to the brown brick complex of the City of London Boys' School,

Blackfriars Station in the process of being extended across Blackfriars Bridge. Circular Space House on Kingsway appears directly in front of the BT Tower.

a couple of bright green football pitches are tucked into the corner created by the 'L'-shaped grey concrete walls of Baynard House. The one visible road – that ramp down to the Embankment – is in front, while the only other green expanses to be seen from here are the green slime embankment walls visible when the tide is low.

Above and beyond, one immediately identifiable icon is the grey dome of the Old Bailey's tower near St Paul's with the glinting gold statue of Justice on top. But unless seen from this angle and height, how many people would know that what appears at street level to be a classical building has a quirky Gothic steep-pitched roof just like the one above the Gothic, church-like nave of its 'brother-in-law' – the Royal Courts of Justice – at the other end of Fleet Street?

On the west side of Blackfriars Bridge stands the white stone curved front of Unilever House with its curved colonnade. Lack of space in the City prompted the creation of the hanging rooftop gardens just visible on top. Above its tree-covered roof on the skyline, a four-turreted tower appears exactly like a miniature version of the Tower of London's White Tower. It belongs to the old Public Records Office, (now the Maughan Library of Kings College) which stands about half a mile away between Fetter and Chancery Lanes.

Trace the view beyond to the left and in the distance the top floors of a grey, circular cake-shaped 1960s building, Space House on Kingsway, stand out. From this angle the BT Tower, situated about a mile behind it, looks like a candle set in the middle of its roof. To the left of Kingsway are the stunted blocks of a stone tower of Freemason's Hall; further left again, a dazzling orange-coloured slice of top-floor flat marks the south-facing façade of Renzo Piano's Central St Giles complex. In front by Temple are the luminous green curved roofs of the British American Tobacco building.

To the left is the new Blackfriars railway station, built on the bridge in a revival of an ancient London tradition, its ticket concourse encased in glass with white tubular bars in a cross-hatching pattern that reaches the roof at the bridge's northeast entrance. All across Blackfriars Bridge the station and trainshed roof has been built in a sawtooth profile to accommodate solar panels.

NORTHEAST

Height restrictions in the City inevitably mean new buildings' footprints are huge; whole blocks of streets must be demolished for an economically viable single new build. Across the Thames from here and to the east, on a gentle upward slope, a whole hub of new buildings around Cannon Street has appeared over the last three years. Each single new office block we see has replaced at least two or three smaller ones from an earlier era, illustrating how profoundly the scale of City new-builds has changed. The black louvre-covered Walbrook building looks like a giant shiny crouching crustacean that has just swallowed up the three old office blocks on the corner of Walbrook and Cannon Street, while from this height it is clear just how far its new neighbour above Cannon Street Station, Cannon Place, has crept down and colonised Dowgate Hill behind. Even One New Change beside the east end of St Paul's has spread the wings of its brown fritted glass wings to encompass several whole streets. Its architect, Jean Nouvel, compensated the City by opening up new walkways inside its arcade.

St Paul's beyond the Millennium Bridge. The red brick building on the Embankment is City of London Boys' School.

THE SKYLON AT THE ROYAL FESTIVAL HALL

A CALM YET COMMANDING VIEW OF THE BUILDINGS LINING THE THAMES, REVEALING A LONDON COMFORTABLE WITH ITSELF

The venue name The Skylon is a tribute to the futuristic cigar-shaped steel and aluminium sculpture that became the emblem of the Festival of Britain, held in the summer of 1951 on the south bank of the Thames. In austere post-Second World War Britain the festival was planned to rejuvenate spirits. The Skylon was 300ft tall, lit from within and stood outside the new Festival Hall, built as the event's centrepiece. It was demolished after the Festival, but the building designed to house London's most prestigious concert hall is now home to a new Skylon – an elegant grill, bar and restaurant. With a triple height north-facing window that overlooks the walkway by the river, the Skylon exudes a suitably cool atmosphere with its off-white exposed structural columns and 1950s-style bronze-coloured circular chandeliers.

Address SE1 8XX
Nearest Tube Waterloo
Open To The Public? Prior booking needed
Disabled accessibility Yes
Website www.skylon-restaurant.co.uk
Contact details 020 7654 7800

The spirit of the original Skylon lives on right outside the window in the white pylons of the new Hungerford Bridge, splaying out from the outward-leaning poles along its walkway. At dusk it is illuminated from the top down, giving it a ghostly but magical sculptural look. Sitting up at the bar close to the window at no great height, this calm yet commanding view across the Thames reveals a London comfortable with how it has become over the years since the end of the Second World War.

NORTHWEST

For the most part the view is not much changed since the Festival of Britain – apart from the cleaner looking stone of the building façades opposite. The only new elephant on the Embankment is the post-modern, pinkish Embankment Place with its double-barrelled vaulted glass-fronted roofs one behind the other, looking like a telescope with protruding ears either side. Yet even that looks comfortably bedded in, despite its bulk, over Charing Cross Station. It is striking how London looks so mature from here and able to handle anything 20th-and 21st-century architects throw at it. Perhaps that is because Embankment Place more than squares up in bulk to its neighbouring 'non-identical twins' to the right, the 1930s New Adelphi and Shell Mex House in white Portland stone. The New Adelphi is a block 'W' in shape with flags on all corners at roof level and inset deep-relief stone sculptures on the corners closer to the ground. Shell Mex House is the angular head-and-shoulders building next door, topped off with a clock tower that looks as if it belongs on a giant's mantelpiece.

Set back slightly with gardens in front of it, the Savoy Hotel stands next in line along the Embankment, looking distinctly more house-like than its neighbours to the left with its long green mansard roof dotted by attic windows. It pre-dates its white stone 'twin' neighbours by about 50 years and was a 'studio' to Impressionist artist Claude Monet while its right-hand neighbour was being built. In contrasting red brick with white stone coursework, the Savoy's next-door neighbour is the Institute of Electrical Engineers. Invisible to the naked eye from here but fairly prominent walking along the Victoria Embankment Gardens is a bronze statue in front of it of pioneer Michael Faraday.

Without leaves on the trees on this side of the river it is easier to spot, in front of Shell Mex House, the Egyptian pale pink granite obelisk on the opposite embankment known as

The tall picture windows of Skylon at the Festival Hall afford superb vistas across the Thames.

Somerset House is immediately east of Waterloo Bridge on the north bank.

Cleopatra's Needle. It dates from 1500 BC, making it London's oldest outdoor monument, but was only imported in 1877. With all the manoeuvring needed to install its 180-ton weight, no one noticed that sculptor George Vulliamy's purpose-built sphinxes, intended to guard the obelisk, were mistakenly placed facing each other and not back-to-back.

NORTH

The view from the Skylon bar is framed on either side by two palaces. To the right, just beyond Waterloo Bridge, is the majestic 18th century Palladian-style Somerset House, built for the civil service by William Chambers on land owned originally by the Dukes of Somerset. Today it houses, among others, the Courtauld Institute's art collection and part of King's College University of London. A pediment and colonnade marks its magnificent Thames-facing entrance, sited on a public walkway high above

river and street level. Below, visible under the arches of Waterloo Bridge, is the palace's original river entrance arch for barges. That now fronts the Victoria Embankment road, indicating how much wider the Thames' waters would have been before the Embankment was built.

WEST

On the extreme left of the view is the palatial Whitehall Court, which can be glimpsed through the spokes of Hungerford Bridge. From the river banks at this distance it looks like the prettiest palace ever designed for London, a fairytale chateau with its multitude of rooftop turrets and spires, wrought-iron balconies and stonework loggias. It was in fact a purpose-built block of superior flats constructed right next door to the Ministry of Defence; behind its innocence a vicious secret spy network was housed through two world wars.

LONDON EYE

A THRILLING WORK OF KINETIC ART SEEN FROM THE 'EYE' OF THE CAPITAL

As the Millennium Wheel, the London Eye was hoisted into position from the Thames to celebrate the year 2000. Today it is owned and run by EDF Energy, Britain's largest electricity generator. Expected to survive as a one-year-only attraction, it worked its way into everyone's affections and has gained an indefinite lease of life. At its highest point the wheel is 443ft tall. It is suspended over the south bank of the Thames by an A frame located on land by the river between Waterloo and Westminster Bridges. When boarding the Eye, visitors know their journey starts from the 'eye' of the capital.

Address Westminster Bridge Road, SE1 7PB
Nearest Tube Waterloo
Open To The Public? Winter; 10am-8:30pm. Summer; 10am-9pm
Disabled accessibility Yes
Website www.londoneye.com

As the Eye turns, London's skyline becomes a thrilling work of kinetic art to be viewed in an anticlockwise direction from one of 32 pod-shaped glass galleries attached to its external edge. The higher a pod rises, the more the city sculpture unravels before your eyes. The wheel's slow-motion rotation changes the viewpoint and view from moment to moment. For a few moments at the top a 360-degree panorama is fully open on all sides of the capsule. Even the most jaded London eyes can be refreshed after a 30-minute revolution. And on a clear day 30 minutes can seem like 30 seconds.

ASCENT

It makes sense to look towards the river downstream on the ascent because the pods ahead and behind are not then in your line of vision. The reverse is true for the descent. Looking east at takeoff, it is only evident as the Thames starts to fall away what a sharp curve of river divides Westminster from the City. As your bearings become clear, overviews of unfamiliar aspects like the wavy extended trainshed of Waterloo station, built for the old Eurostar, or the green curve of the Royal Festival Hall's roof are distractions from all the famous landmarks starting to appear. These early moments prepare the eyes for new knowledge of old places.

The white bulk of the former Shell Centre dominates the foreground.

Moving to the capsule's northeast corner, suddenly the vista bursts open. Whole swathes of east London like the dome of St Paul's, utterly invisible at takeoff, 'rise up' to identify where the City and, a moment later, Canary Wharf belong in this grand sculpture of Greater London. In the northeast the massive white roof of the Emirates Stadium appears above the conurbation of Highbury like a spaceship out of the blue. All the while the Royal National Theatre and neighbouring halls begin to line themselves up along the Thames' Jubilee Walkway below on the Southbank.

By now there is an uninterrupted view across the Thames of the Charles Barry and Augustus Pugin's neo-Gothic Palace of Westminster, a star of Victorian engineering built on a dam right over the river. The view is still intimate enough to identify how the Palace's neighbour, the gloriously Gothic façade of Henry VII's Chapel at the eastern end of Westminster Abbey, wholly inspired Pugin's design roughly 340 years later.

As the Eye nears its climactic full height, the view of Westminster's homes to government begins to take on a majestic appeal even from this bird's-eye height. The north range of Whitehall's offices, including the Admiralty, Scottish Office and Cabinet Office, appear almost like an impenetrable citadel wall along the length of Westminster's widest street. By the time the pod begins its descent, the decorative white stone façades of the Treasury and Foreign Office buildings have exposed the immensely deep inner courtyards, surrounded by layers of offices, behind their forbidding walls.

In between them the narrow 'alley' of Downing Street, with its black iron gates and toytown policemen just about visible in front and behind, leads to the massive beige gravel expanse of Horseguards Parade spread out in front of St James's Park. The park, and its curved man-made lake with tree-filled bird sanctuary islands, appears somehow thickly wooded from here. Its rural aspect makes the tree-lined Mall, shooting straight alongside, look like a super-sized empty highway leading up to a doll's house Buckingham Palace at its northwest end.

DESCENT

Having shrunk into insignificance inside central London's urban density, Nelson's Column starts to rise again to the northeast. Even the early town planning of John Nash's processional route from the Mall through Regent Street to Regent's Park can just be defined as the pod descends. Crowds straight down below on Westminster Bridge are visible now, as are the distant towers of Brentford crowding around the A4 as it passes Gunnersbury Park.

All five Thames bridges visible during the ride – Vauxhall, Lambeth,

Westminster, Hungerford and Waterloo – come into view looking down through the Eye's wheel spokes. Hungerford's sets of gathered white steel cables look like rows of pluckable stringed instruments that could belong in the Royal Festival Hall.

Looking southwest at the river curve by Vauxhall Bridge, St George's Wharf – a row of five glass residential pavilion piers with pastel green roofs – descends in height and in rows to the riverbank. It totally upstages the vapid post-modern 'citadel' of MI6, its riverside neighbour, on this side of the bridge. Alongside MI6 is the faintly notorious Peninsula Heights, London home to many a Westminster Lord, the black glass tower standing out with its white corner balconies.

The last memory of rooftops as the Eye reaches home base is the crescent-shaped steep red-tiled roof with central green lantern of County Hall, formerly the home of London's government.

Two of the five bridges – Hungerford and Waterloo – visible from the London Eye.

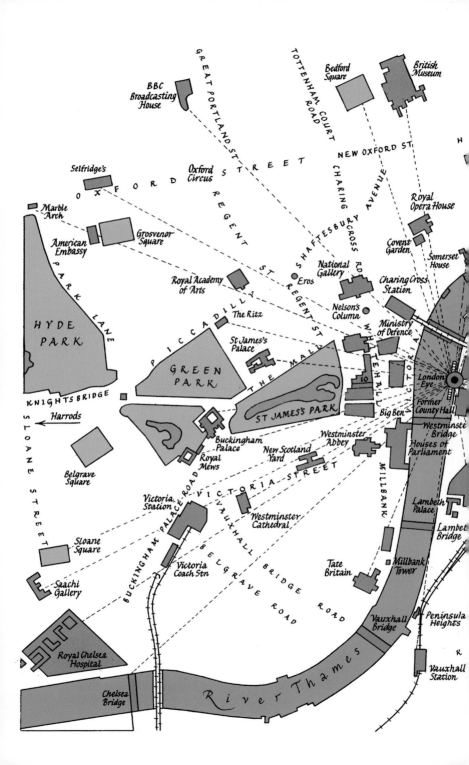

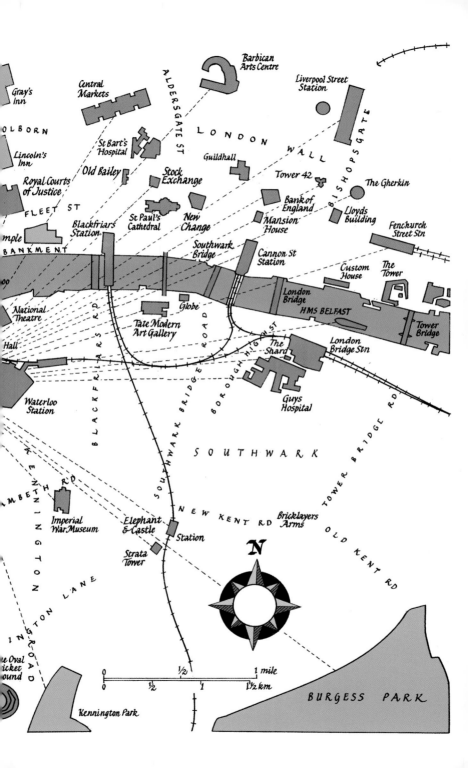

ALTITUDE 360 AT MILLBANK TOWER

A BIRD'S-EYE VIEW OF THE THAMES IN SOUTHWEST LONDON

This bulge of land surrounded by the River Thames was once a swampy marsh, known since Henry VIII's day for water fowl hunting. Early in the 19th century, speculative builders aiming to fulfil the housing demands of London's new middle class took full advantage of the engineering genius of Thomas Cubitt, the man responsible for draining the land ready for building. The office block known as Millbank Tower, built 150 years later on the site of a vast penitentiary from which transported prisoners were forced to embark for the long voyage to Australia, has given over its top five floors to events venue Altitude. The topmost floor is known as Altitude 360.

Address 21-24 Millbank, SW1P 4QP
Nearest Tube Vauxhall
Open To The Public? Private hire
Disabled accessibility Yes
Website www.altitudelondon.com
Contact details 0845 500 2929

 From this height we become aware that Millbank Tower stands near the tip of what is quite plainly a peninsula. Looking over the shape of the land, the surprise is how easily our street-level mindset misleads us as to the physical reality of this busy area at the heart of the borough of Westminster. Vauxhall Bridge Road is not a north-south arterial route from Victoria to the River Thames, as most drivers would imagine, but traverses Pimlico from northwest to southeast. The river explains it all from up here.

EAST

Looking from the southeast-facing window on the 29th floor, the Thames flows downstream and disappears past the Houses of Parliament around the bulge of Southwark. Behind Westminster Bridge, the London Eye takes centre stage. In the foreground of the view, the Archbishop of Canterbury's home, Lambeth Palace, just across red Lambeth Bridge, looks more impressive than from the street. Behind those protective walls is a complex of ancient stone and Tudor red-brick buildings with towers, crenellated battlements and flags, surrounded by a substantial piece of land. On the opposite side of the road from the Palace, the buildings of St Thomas' Hospital line the south bank of the river. Architecturally they are so diverse they look totally disconnected from one another, as if not part of the same institution. The most eye-catching in the complex is the Evelina Children's Hospital, its braced glass barrelled roof supported by bright terracotta-orange structural bands.

SOUTH

Continuing south, the Thames flows upstream under Vauxhall Bridge, beyond which the dramatic curves of the Oval cricket ground are visible. The river vanishes as it curves around the peninsular bulge where we stand. MI6 on the southwest side of Vauxhall Bridge is the beige stone fortress with opaque green windows.

The southwest window overlooks Tate Britain immediately below with its central cupola. An impressive feature at ground level, from up here it is almost lost among the roofs of six additional annexes added behind the main building since the 1930s.

A miniature parade quadrangle is surrounded by the remains of the old Army and Medical College built at the turn of the 20th century. One pretty building just below us facing the Thames is the old Mess Rooms, restored and rebuilt for Chelsea College of Art and Design. North of the quadrangle some of the original octagonal plan of the Millbank Penitentiary, built on this site in 1816, is discernible in the radial street pattern.

On the south bank, after the green and fawn tower complex of St George's Wharf that descends like a series of broad staircases down to the riverbank (and the new tower block beside under construction), the river landscape becomes suddenly very industrial with its waste recovery barges and refuse collection facilities.

The Thames sweeping eastwards, with Lambeth Palace far right.

West along the north bank from Altitude. The strip of red brick is the Millbank Estate.

NORTH

From Millbank Tower's east window, the twin MI5 Thames House buildings immediately below are revealed to possess central oblong-shaped atriums on their roofs – but nothing more exciting than that. Beyond them and close to Parliament Square the buildings of Whitehall and Westminster appear tightly bunched together – even the landmark Abbey is not easily picked out. Looking further northwards, the West End is a dense urban mass, even from this height; only the moving bright lights of a LED-lit advertising screen on the corner of Haymarket and Coventry Street peeping between the grey stone buildings provide an orientation spot.

WEST

The north-facing window gives an insider's close-up of Westminster 'suburbia'. In the distance the local playing fields of Vincent Square stand out in green. Nearby the view is dominated by two adjacent but architecturally contrasting housing estates. Immediately below on John Islip Street is the Millbank Estate. The early 20th century council flats in red brick, with white render terraces under steep pitched roofs, look from here like quaint toytown buildings. Almost adjoining to the right is the 1920s Grosvenor Estate, a sea of flat roofs over five-storey blocks. Their eye-catching chequerboard walls, in alternating rectangles of window, grey brick and off-white render, go down to meet a little pavilion-shaped shop at each ground level entrance. Looking to the western side of the peninsula, the elegant rows of Cubitt's white stucco terraces stand facing the Thames. Further west still, the symmetrical rows of housing blocks at right angles to the river belong to the gigantic post-Second World War Churchill Gardens Estate.

Diagonally across the top floor from the northwest-facing windows, the view picks up the River Thames again on the left after it has completed its dramatic curve. From this side, Chelsea, Albert and Battersea bridges stretch out to the west with a good view of Battersea Power Station before the curve of SW6 takes the Thames out of view again – this time for good.

HENMAN HILL

A UNIQUE INTRODUCTION TO LONDON'S LANDMARKS, RANGED ALONG THE BANKS OF THE UNSEEN THAMES

Correctly known, according to the All England Lawn Tennis Club, as the Aorangi Picnic Terrace, the picnic tables and kiosks on this artificial hill face a 430 square foot screen during the Championships. In 1997, the year of the hill's creation from spoil excavated due to the resiting of Court One, British favourite Tim Henman was aiming to reach the final; his supporters congregated here to watch his progress on the screen, which thus gained its popular nickname. The area had once been leased to the New Zealand Rugby Club, and when the rugby posts were removed the memory of that period was enshrined in the Maori name Aorangi, which means 'Cloud in the Sky' – appropriate to normal Championships weather but actually the original name of Mount Cook.

Address Church Road, SW19 5AE
Nearest Tube Southfields
Open To The Public? Strictly timed tours
Disabled accessibility Yes
Website www.oeltc.com
Contact details 020 8946 2244

Rain may stop play at the Wimbledon Championships, but rain at all other times clears the city air to present one of the most dynamic views of London from the very top of Henman Hill. On a tour of the club, the focus from here is on the southerly view where the Wimbledon parish church of St Mary's sits dramatically perched on the brow surrounded by trees, with nothing but more trees visible beyond. St Mary's was established in Saxon times, thus pre-dating the game of tennis and this world-famous club by around 1250 years.

But with central London separated from the All England Lawn Tennis Club by roughly 12 miles, the clarity of the view east from the wooden bridge over the ornamental stream that runs across the top of Henman Hill is even more surprising. It offers a unique range of landmarks standing in a row all along the banks of the unseen Thames. For those visiting London for the first time, it presents a distorted but perfect series of all London's 'must see' buildings, standing in an orderly row from left to right.

Starting on the extreme left, the London Eye curves up like a triumphal arch straddling two central London tower blocks. The Houses of Parliament's iconic 316ft clock tower nestles immediately in front of it and slightly to the left. As Londoners should know, it is the bell inside

and not the clock that we call Big Ben. It was named after a tall civil engineer, Benjamin Hall – the first Commissioner of the Metropolitan Board of Works. The installation of the 14-ton bell in St Stephen's Tower was just a tiny part of the entire rebuilding of the Palace of Westminster in the mid 19th century.

The frequent breaks between games and sets are to give time to admire the distant view.

Direct your eyes to the right of the clock tower and adjacent to it the upturned four white table-leg towers of Battersea Power Station are easily identified. This monumental Grade II* listed brick and concrete structure was London's largest coal-burning power station, creating electricity for London for over 50 years until 1983 when it was decommissioned. Today it is a declining shadow of its former self, bought by a series of speculative

The whole London skyline from the southwest – Battersea to Docklands.

developers who have been unable to realise their plans and sold it on. But, at least for now, it remains immortalised in its heyday adorning the cover of the 1977 Pink Floyd album, *Animals*, with a pink inflatable pig in flight above it. The bright blue water pumping tower a short way from Battersea Power Station is itself Grade II listed, but its future too continues to hang in the balance. So far the various developers' plans for this iconic riverside site have not included preserving the water tower.

Perversely from this height and angle, the City of London stands next in line to the right of Battersea's four chimneys. The giant rocket silhouette of the Gherkin, its neighbour Tower 42 and the new Heron Tower are clustered together looking as if they stand just behind the trees of Wimbledon Park in the foreground. In full leaf these trees almost obscure London's tallest new icon, the Shard, giving new prominence to the south side of London Bridge where the building's nozzle pokes out above the trees.

At a very slight distance to the right from the Shard and competing with the new giant's quirky profile stands south London's other new skyline signature residential building, the stripey black and white Strata tower at Elephant and Castle, the three giant turbines on its roof framed on a really clear day.

Looking to the right, very little stands out against the sky until the right-hand corner of the view, where a cluster of remote greyish giants appear faintly threatening in isolation as they dominate the skyline, dwarfing any building nearby. Standing at the centre of this group, unmistakable with a piercing light blinking from its pyramid-shaped silver rooftop (even at this distance of approximately 13 miles) is Number One Canada Square. Since it was planned in 1982 this building has become synonymous with the name of Canary Wharf, the sleek hub housing the world's international financial markets developed out of the rotting old West India Docks on the northern edge of the Isle of Dogs peninsula.

WESTMINSTER CATHEDRAL BELL TOWER

THE BEGINNER'S GUIDE TO LONDON'S SKYLINE

The late 19th-century Byzantine-style Westminster Cathedral was built in the heart of Victoria as the centre of England's Roman Catholic faith. The church complex is remarkable from both inside and out, and its 284ft high rectangular campanile or bell tower offers a perfect four-sided vista that could be dubbed 'the beginner's guide to London's skyline'. A lift inside the tower's core travels up to the seventh floor where four tiny Italian loggia-style covered balconies, one on each side of the tower, simplify London's vast expanse. The floor above houses the church bell, St Edward, under the cupola roof.

Address 42 Francis Street, SW1 1QW

Nearest Tube Victoria

Open To The Public? Mon-Fri 9:30am-5:00pm, Weekends/hols 9:30am-6:00pm; entrance fee

Disabled accessibility Yes

Website www.westminstercathedral.org.uk

Contact details 020 7798 9005

SOUTH

Step out on to the south balcony and the cathedral's three massive green copper domes just below are an immediate and stunning surprise. Rows of red-brick mansion flats of similar height dominate the streets either side of the church. Bands of white stone contrasting with the red brick make the slim domed turrets that punctuate both sides of the nave walls stand out sharply. This 'blood and bandage' effect brickwork complements the white stone window mullions of those neighbouring flats.

Just beyond the flats is Vincent Square, with playing fields for Westminster School, and to the left of it the rather blackened yellow brick spire of St Stephen's Church. Their existence lends a villagey atmosphere to the Victoria area despite the presence of its busy station hub.

Between Victoria and the Thames, Pimlico's white stucco terraces with their unadorned London stock brick backs range down to Vauxhall Bridge, where on this side of the Thames the 1960s glass tower, Riverwalk House, is earmarked for replacement. Slightly to the west the residential quadrangle of citadel-like Dolphin Square and the yellow brick geometric residential blocks of Churchill Gardens estate dominate the north bank along Grosvenor Road.

The Thames is hidden. But along the south bank's Albert Embankment newer buildings such as Peninsula Heights, MI6, St George's Wharf and high-rise circular Vauxhall Tower have brought this area, Nine Elms, back into developers' focus. Thanks to its proximity to Westminster, this hitherto neglected stretch is to be linked with neighbouring Battersea Power Station for wholesale regeneration.

In the far distance the Crystal Palace transmission tower on Sydenham Hill lines up almost parallel to the Croydon transmitter on Beulah Hill in South Norwood.

EAST

From the east-facing balcony, a broad span of a view includes the Strata on the south bank to the right, and Canary Wharf to Westminster and the City to the left. On a clear day the vista reveals Shooters Hill and the hills of Sidcup and Bexleyheath, around 17 miles away.

The densely packed conglomeration of landmark buildings results in a rather indifferent, but unusual sighting of both Westminster Abbey and St Paul's Cathedral in a single view. St Paul's is virtually camouflaged, while closer by the pale Westminster Abbey appears to have the lantern of the Palace of Westminster's Clock Tower behind,

The Eye peeps above Transport for London's brown granite offices to the east; the Palace of Westminster's Victoria tower sees off the Shard.

The 'blood and bandage' brickwork of the surrounding mansion flats and two of the Cathedral's three domes fill the view from the south balcony.

protruding from the left-hand tower of its own western entrance. Until a couple of decades ago these two religious icons would have stood out, but without present laws to protect sightlines their importance in this view has diminished. However the Palace's Victoria Tower takes its revenge on their behalf by shielding the new Shard from a full-on view. The Gherkin is the orientation highlight for the City today.

The middle distance is partially obscured by a 1970s brownish polished granite building with a façade of triangular bays. Housing the offices of Transport for London, it appears to have the top segment of the London Eye poking out above its roof and the grey slate tiled roof of Methodist Central Hall attached to its left façade.

NORTH

To the extreme right the view overlaps with Centre Point. In the foreground, a 1960s white concrete-framed glass block with blue blinds in the windows and a Union Jack flying from the roof is the headquarters of Westminster City Council on Victoria Street. To the left of it, in eye-catchingly bright terracotta colour with a silver-grey penthouse on top, is Wellington House, a new residential flatiron-shaped building on Buckingham Gate.

Harrow, with the lower ranges of the Chilterns in Buckinghamshire visible beyond.

WEST

The surprisingly broad span of Victoria Station's trainshed roof is in the foreground. A pair of domes with curious bright green finials on top adorn the grey fish-scale tiled roof of the Grosvenor Hotel attached to the west side of the station. These domes match the bulbous French Renaissance tiled roofs of elegant Parisian-looking apartment houses visible beyond, surrounding adjacent Grosvenor Gardens. This little corner of London is often thought to be its most 'French', a quality keenly discernible from up here.

Facing due west, the busy view spans a collection of landmark towers. From right to left they are Knightsbridge Barracks (currently shrouded in scaffolding) at the south of Hyde Park, where the Life Guards' horses are stabled on the first and second level with the soldiers living above, Imperial College's white Victoria Tower with green cupola, the far distant silhouette of the Southall water tower, the V&A dome, the grey factory-like roof of Earl's Court exhibition centre, the Empress State Building, and the tower of the Grosvenor Pumping Station where Chelsea Bridge over the Thames is partially visible.

Straight ahead the white Nash terraces on the north side of the Mall face St James's Park. Slightly to the left Clarence House peeps out from behind the trees. Further to the left, at the end of the Mall, the Victoria Memorial fronts the rooftops of Buckingham Palace and Green Park behind. Turning to the far left, beyond the left-hand side of Portland House in the immediate foreground, are the trees of Hyde Park – three Royal Parks in one view.

Leaving the countless rebuilding and retrofitting sites in the foreground on Victoria Street, in the middle distance the BT Tower eclipses the Euston Tower with the hills of Highgate and Hampstead in the far distance. At the left-hand 'corner' of the view the arch of Wembley Stadium fronts the distant hills of

LONDON HILTON ON PARK LANE

CONTRASTING EAST AND WEST LONDON FROM A FASHIONABLE 1960S VIEWPOINT

The Galvin at Windows on the 28th floor of the Park Lane Hilton has a bar with stunning views of London to the west and east. This was London's first Hilton hotel, opened with a much-publicised restaurant on top in 1963. A veritable skyscraper in the day, it was a novelty as one of the very few chic spaces open to the public that could show off the skyline of Swinging London out below.

Address 22 Park Lane, W1K 1BE
Nearest Tube Hyde Park Corner
Open To The Public? Prior booking needed for restaurant
Disabled accessibility Yes
Website www.galvinatwindows.com
Contact details 020 7208 4021

EAST

Those viewing east London from Windows have undoubtedly seen drastic changes in the skyline since this hotel opened. The city looks packed with a wild variety of shapes and heights; famous attractions like Nelson's Column and the magnificent west entrance of St Paul's blend into the unremarkable, sunk into insignificance behind a monumental brown brick prison of a nearby structure. Called Berkeley Square House, it occupies the entire length of the square's west side.

The bar's east window has its share of signature attractions, including the humpback basketball arena at the Olympic Park. But with no open space for breath, the view lacks rhythm; instead, colours train the eye. The bright citrus-coloured façade panels of the new Central St Giles complex next to Centre Point stand out. Green cupolas bob up here and there, along with the green of the Ministry of Defence roof and County Hall's green bell tower, and to their left bright green glass buildings like that of medical charity the Wellcome Trust, with its massive slice of sloping glass roof. The building cranes themselves seem to multiply as we look, indicating there is no letup in sight for east London's expansion.

WEST

Now head for the windows opposite where the attractions lie in the mature and relatively calm low-lying view over west London. The gentle geometric layout of Hyde Park's south side immediately before us is unexpectedly soothing. Straight rows of trees line the soft orange-brown bridleway of Rotten Row where it passes alongside a bulging southern edge of the Serpentine. From here we can see exactly where Joseph Paxton built his Crystal Palace for the Great Exhibition of 1851 on the expanse of grass between Rotten Row and the other parallel rows of trees lining the park's carriage drive, though not a ghost of it now remains.

Where Rotten Row ends, an internal road divides Hyde Park from adjoining Kensington Gardens. Just beyond and straight ahead is the seated golden figure of Albert in his Memorial, leaning slightly forward in profile to face his other memorial – the Royal Albert Hall. Just outside the Park, the Albert Hall is defined from here only by its shallow domed glass roof. Below us, at the start of Rotten Row, is Hyde Park Corner roundabout; in its centre is the white stone triumphal arch, topped with the statue of winged Victory, commemorating

Centre Point rears up to the east, with the splash of colour from the new Central St Giles development.

The monumental brown edifice of Berkeley Square house is foreground right; the green mirror-glass of University College Hospital tower and the Wellcome Trust beside the BT Tower to the distant left.

the Battle of Waterloo. Facing the roundabout on the edge of the park we look down on the top of the victorious Duke of Wellington's home, Apsley House, half of its roof clad in shining copper.

More immediately below and to the southwest Grosvenor Crescent's tall, elegant town houses gently round the curve into white stucco-covered Belgrave Square, just discernible by the clumps of trees in its garden. With its contemporary white classical columns, the Lanesborough Hotel faces Hyde Park Corner, closing off Grosvenor Crescent at this end.

To the left of Hyde Park Corner roundabout, between Constitution Hill and Grosvenor Place, can be glimpsed the northwest corner of Buckingham Palace garden. Located far from the Palace itself and surrounded by foliage, this corner contains a solitary hard tennis court in an obvious state of abandon, as if confirming the Queen's preference for horse-related rather than racket-based sport.

Another major hotel just a stone's throw away, beyond Hyde Park Corner in the direction of Knightsbridge, is the concrete circular drum-like tower of the Sheraton Park Tower. From here it looks as if Harrods' terracotta dome is sticking out from its left side. The grey lead dome of the church called the Oratory of St Philip Neri, but better known as the Brompton Oratory, rises from the centre of its flat roof with the top part of the neighbouring V&A's open-dome crown roof visible directly behind it.

To the right of the Sheraton are the four brand new glass pavilions side by side of Number One Hyde Park – London's most expensive apartment complex. Attractive for investment, almost all the units are taken though fewer than ten per cent are permanently occupied.

SOUTHWEST

Only a tiny stretch of the Thames is visible, further to the southwest where it curves beside Chelsea Harbour Pier with the Overground railway bridge crossing the Thames in the background and the steep pyramid-shaped roof of the Belvedere Tower, part of Chelsea Harbour marina's residential complex, on the north bank.

To its immediate right the decommissioned Lots Road Power Station sticks up two fingers to the four towers of Battersea Power Station on the south bank. Further right, the stylish and angular Empress State Building and the rectangular glass tower of the Earl's Court Holiday Inn flank a grey bunker-type structure with hipped roof, the main hall of Earl's Court exhibition centre.

NORTHWEST

Behind and beyond the nearby tower of Knightsbridge Barracks, some of the suburban towers of the North Circular Road become distinguishable on a very clear day. Past Alperton, Park Royal and out to Wembley, distant London suddenly becomes a rural village with the spire of St Mary's 12 miles away quietly rising at Harrow on the Hill.

Hyde Park's Rotten Row to the west, with Apsley House in the lefthand corner.

WATERSTONES 5TH VIEW

AN OVERSIGHT OF WESTMINSTER AMID ART DECO OPULENCE

One of the era's most progressively designed buildings, the five-storey Waterstones bookshop on Piccadilly was built in 1936 for its former tenant, menswear store Simpson's. On street level the store pioneered a new sales technique: a wide span frame of arc-welded steel permitting an uninterrupted length of shop front either side of the canopied main entrance. The unique curved glazing, designed to reduce reflections for the window browser, was another breakthrough idea. The view from the south side windows of the fifth-floor restaurant and bar, aptly named 5th View, is a treat.

Address 203-205 Piccadilly Lane W1J 9LE
Nearest Tube Piccadilly Circus
Open To The Public? Yes
Disabled accessibility Yes
Website www.5thview.co.uk
Contact details 020 7851 2433

It is tempting to take the original open-plan staircase up to the fifth floor to appreciate the soft interior design lines and the 1930s chrome door and light fittings. Entering 5th View, the space is divided: the lounge side of the bar has deep armchairs below a window that faces the Piccadilly rooftops to the north. Around the other side of the floor a good-size picture window faces south.

SOUTHEAST

The first skyline landmarks from the left-hand corner of the window are a peek of the Shard's peak and a sliver of the very top of St Martin-in-the-Fields' perforated clock tower. Through some anti-pigeon netting over the roof just outside it is possible to catch a glimpse in profile of the very top of Elephant and Castle's black and white Strata tower with its three turbines. To the left, a bigger grey slate roof on Jermyn Street obscures all but about the top 35 degrees of the London Eye. Next to that, the top six storeys and penthouse of New Zealand House rise above this same roof.

The view of the Victoria Tower of Charles Barry and Augustus Pugin's Palace of Westminster, however, takes centre stage from this window. This is the sovereign's entrance to the Houses of Parliament, marking the Palace's extreme west side. Because from this height not even the roof of the Palace is visible, the much smaller spikey Central Tower to the Victoria Tower's left, over the Central Lobby, does not appear related to it. Further to the left we see only a tiny section of the Clock Tower, containing Big Ben. From here we can just catch the sleek pyramid-shaped tiled top of the tower with its gold finial. Since 1885 the lantern close to the top has housed the Ayrton Light, which shines at night when either house is still sitting.

In the foreground, an office block at close range divides the silhouettes of the Big Ben Clock Tower to the right and the 14ft high memorial statue of the Duke of York against the sky to the left. Just to the right of the Houses of Parliament there is a clear view of the tower, transept and nave roofs of 13th and 14th century Westminster Abbey and the two bright white early 18th century tower additions, designed by Nicholas Hawksmoor, that frame the west entrance. The abbey rooftops are surprisingly light in colour. To the right, on a hill in the far distance, stand two transmission towers – the smaller Crystal Palace transmitter to the left and the Croydon transmitter to the right. At dusk both light up, adding to the thrill of the view. In between them, much closer, stands the Millbank Tower on the north bank of the Thames.

SOUTH

Back in Westminster, the charcoal-grey lantern of Methodist Central

Hall's roof appears to stand just to the right of the Crystal Palace transmitter, with an adjacent view of a rooftop array of aerials that identify New Scotland Yard's glass building on Victoria Street. In front sit three massive and curiously shaped white blocks with squat roofs and a bulky tower on the left-hand side. These make up the Home Office, built in the 1970s and located between St James's Park and the attractive Georgian houses near St James's Park Underground station. From this angle they appear far more intrusive on the neighbourhood than at street level.

The view further west (or to the right) is quickly redeemed by Westminster Cathedral's magnificent square Italianate campanile on the northwest corner. Its red brick and stone dressings stripe upward all the way to its little stone grey domed roof, surmounted by an 11ft high cross – containing a supposed relic of the True Cross – which is barely visible to the naked eye from here.

The towers of Westminster's Abbey and Palace to the left; Westminster Cathedral's tower far right

THE NATIONAL PORTRAIT GALLERY RESTAURANT

A LUNCHTIME VIEW OF LONDON'S MAJOR ATTRACTIONS

The National Portrait Gallery houses Britain's collection of images of historically important men and women in a Florentine Renaissance-style building opened in 1895. The restaurant on its uppermost floor is a favourite lunchtime haunt of art critics and arts journalists. The view from the lengthy south-facing window offers a landscape mural – a pleasant relief from viewing numerous faces close-up in the galleries below.

Address St. Martin's Place, WC2H 0HE
Nearest Tube Charing Cross
Open To The Public? Private hire
Disabled accessibility Yes
Website www.npg.org.uk
Contact details 020 7312 2419

From the modest height of the restaurant's picture window, first-time London visitors can familiarise themselves with the capital's most popular tourist destinations on a virtual tour over lunch. The abutting rooftop expanse of William Wilkins' 1838 National Gallery lies just outside the window. All Grecian columns and stone grandeur at ground level, from up here the view is dominated by a six-sided glazed lantern, with a chunky rectangular stone turret to the left and surrounded by pitched and ridged opaque glass roofs set at a variety of angles to each other like some low mountain range.

Just when you think you have found a central Westminster view without the London Eye, it appears curving over the right-hand slope of that atrium. Conversely it is impossible not to notice the largest central pepperpot cupola on the National Gallery's rooftop because it sits so close by. Just beyond it up pops Nelson's stone statue, taller than the cupola with only the upper part of its white column visible. Standing with his back to his memorial, Trafalgar Square – albeit constructed 40 years after his great sea victory and death – he seems rather ungrateful.

SOUTHEAST

To the left, so close you almost miss it, is the perforated church tower of St Martin-in-the-Fields. The open-sided belfry just above the clock face reveals the silhouetted bell. The blue clock face with golden numerals and hands is truly stunning at this height. In contrast, just behind the church tower and further to the left, sits the black clock, with dashes not numbers, attached to the central white stone tower of Shell Mex House. In between the two clocks is the huge curved roof of Embankment Place; only one of its wings, protruding at an angle, is visible from here. To the right of that wing we get a clear view of the Shell Centre's stubby pyramid-topped tower, with two flags flying either side, on the south bank of the Thames at Waterloo.

SOUTH

Looking down, the broad street tracking due south from Trafalgar Square is easily identifiable as Whitehall, with many a government department building on either side of it exposed from an unusual angle. The elegant curves of the buildings either side of Northumberland Avenue to the left are a reminder that almost all this part of Westminster, including the Dukes of Northumberland's London residence, was demolished to accommodate these government institutions. On the left-hand side of Whitehall, two beautiful black stone turrets stand out, their stone domes topped with elegant finials. This chunky early 20th century stone building is the Old War Office. Opposite, the copper green domes over William

Kent's Horse Guards roofs (built 150 years earlier) become visible.

Further down the left-hand side of Whitehall, between the Ministry of Defence (easily identified by flags dotted over its roof) and the iconic towers of the Palace of Westminster, it is possible to distinguish contrasting two styles of chimney pot. The first are the stripy red-brick and white stone chimney stacks of the original New Scotland Yard, to which the Metropolitan Police headquarters moved in 1890 (the modern New Scotland Yard, built in 1967 with rotating sign, is on the other side of Parliament Square off Victoria Street). Rising above the great sloping red roof, they reflect Arts and Crafts-influenced architect Norman Shaw's favourite

The central pepperpot cupola of the National Gallery flanks Nelson on his column.

Big Ben is in the distance.

colour-contrasted building materials of the 1890s. The second notable chimneys just beyond Shaw's are the black bronze flues designed by Michael Hopkins as part of the air conditioning services to his Portcullis House, finished in 2001 as overspill offices for Members of Parliament. The Palace of Westminster's three towers provide a focal point where Whitehall ends at Parliament Square on the east side.

SOUTHWEST

To the west we glimpse the tiled, bulging domed roof of Methodist Central Hall, looking distinctly Viennese. Close beside it is New Scotland Yard's tall glass rectangular tower. It is possible to make out the white stone stepped upper reaches of Broadway House, a hefty 1920s 'modern' block by architect Charles Holden that doubles as TfL's headquarters and St James's Park Station.

Drawing our gaze in close, we see the honey-coloured stone of classical Greek-style Canada House, flanking the west side of Trafalgar Square with its row of oval-windowed attic rooms. On the south side sits the Trafalgar Hotel with its square clock turret – originally built for Cunard, it later housed the offices of the Royal Mail Steam Packet Company. Looking along the office tops of Cockspur Street there is an intriguing baroque green copper dome with an openwork globe speared above it, capped with a beautiful gold sailing ship. Once part of the Peninsular and Oriental (P&O) shipping line offices, this building is currently unoccupied. To the right over the jumble of rooftops, an office building roof with a pretty lantern and spire stands out next to the 1960s blue glass 15-storey tower of New Zealand House on Haymarket. It looks very unselfconscious among the Portland stone and stucco of its surroundings.

THE SHERATON PARK TOWER

ARISTOCRATIC WEST LONDON FROM THE HEART OF KNIGHTSBRIDGE

The circular Sheraton Park Tower opened in 1973 as the Skyline Park Tower Hotel, the first modern luxury tower hotel to be constructed in pre-cast concrete. It stands where Knightsbridge meets Belgravia, just a stone's throw from Hyde Park, Harrods, Harvey Nichols and a plethora of brand-name boutiques on Sloane Street. The penthouse suites on the top (17th) floor are named after their views.

Address 101 Knightsbridge, SW1X 7RN
Nearest Tube Knightsbridge
Open To The Public? Only for overnight stay
Disabled accessibility Yes
Website www.sheratontower.com
Contact details 020 7235 8050

From the Lowndes suite's sitting-room window, Lowndes Square – more of a narrow rectangle – can be seen immediately below. It is surrounded by rows of white terraces with columned portico entrances, all facing a strip of central garden so slim it barely figures on maps of the area. The hotel takes up the whole northern side of the square.

From here west London divides into two areas that, since they were built, have always squared up to each other for the accolade of being the most upper class. They are Knightsbridge and Belgravia and this hotel is just inside the Belgravia camp. The ownership of the land of both areas largely remains in the hands of the aristocracy who have passed it down for centuries.

SOUTHEAST

Belgravia is still the domain of the Grosvenor family, entitled the Dukes of Westminster. As is traditional for speculative builders developing new areas of London, the Grosvenors named many of the streets between the main roads of Grosvenor Place and Sloane Street after their country estates. Belgravia is architecturally characterised by tall stucco-faced terraces, mostly situated around squares. To the left of Lowndes, there are rows of white houses around the squares named Belgravia and Eaton but as the view also reveals, the backs of the houses are in the familiar greyish-yellow London brick rather than being plastered with

To the left St Paul's Church on Wilton Place sits at the junction where Belgravia stucco meets Knightsbridge brick.

stucco. Before buildings as high as this one were built, nobody but the neighbours would have been expected to know that.

SOUTHWEST

To the west of Sloane Street, much of Knightsbridge is still owned by the descendants of 18th-century royal physician Sir Hans Sloane. The family names include Cadogan and Stanley. In architectural terms, Knightsbridge is broadly defined by its brick and terracotta-red terraced houses, mostly tall and gabled in Dutch style – without a dollop of stucco in sight.

From the 17th floor Sloane Street itself is decipherable by the modern stone tower of Carlton Tower on the left side, with only a few fronts and rooftops visible opposite. But to the right of Sloane Street tall cliffs of red-brick houses and apartments form straight grid patterns southwards towards Cadogan Square. Closer to home on the right is the red terracotta façade of Harrods as it goes round the corner of Hans Crescent and Basil Street. Its rooftop's iconic terracotta dome and tall industrial chimney stand out among a jumble of small utilities. The sides of the building are so long the whole department store takes up the equivalent space of a few residential streets.

NORTHEAST

Meanwhile, with a pair of decent binoculars, most of central London to the southeast and west is yours as you lie back in the jacuzzi-fitted bath and stare through the floor-to-ceiling window of the master bathroom. The black winged figure of Victory on her

The Sheraton Park Tower

four-horse chariot on the roundabout at Hyde Park Corner stands out against the trees of Buckingham Palace's back garden and Green Park. Although the triumphal arch on which she stands is not visible, with her arms aloft she looks as if she is having a semaphore conversation with her golden-winged sister atop the Victoria Memorial outside Buckingham Palace's Mall entrance, across the treetops to the right. That huge rectangular honey-coloured stone quadrangle beside her is part of the Palace itself.

Beyond Green Park's trees, the skyline fills up with London's best-known shapes: the London Eye, with the Shard silhouetted through its spokes, the Houses of Parliament's Clock Tower and Victoria Tower separated by the finials on the roof of Westminster Abbey, and the Gherkin with fellow City towers to the left. To the left of those, slightly in the foreground, the figure of Nelson on his column at Trafalgar Square and the view of St Paul's directly behind is an interesting compression of locations. In the left-hand corner on the edge of the view is the Park Lane Hilton with Hyde Park and the Duke of Wellington's home, Number One London, in front on the corner. Just squeezing on the extreme left is the tower of Centre Point on Tottenham Court Road.

NORTH

The astonishing size of Hyde Park as seen from the window of the next-door suite takes your breath away. At 350 acres it takes up most of the view from here, justifying its nickname: the lung of London. In front of it, the four brand new glass pavilions of different heights make up Number One Hyde Park; they appear joined at the hip to the Mandarin Oriental Hotel with rear windows overlooking the south side of the park.

From up here the park's walking paths, wide and narrow, across a treeless expanse of grass form a complex grid pattern down to the Serpentine. If the planned Olympic screens face the right way, this suite will be a plum location from which to view the 2012 Games. On the park's north perimeter, new clusters of tall buildings, some triangular in shape, constructed around regenerated Paddington and its Basin now rise behind Bayswater's rows of stucco terraces.

Hyde Park sweeps away to Bayswater on the north side.

TOP FLOOR AT PETER JONES

AN INTIMATE INSIGHT INTO RESIDENTIAL WEST LONDON

Designed with a curve that adjusts to the curve of King's Road, department store Peter Jones at Sloane Square is one of London's first glazed curtain wall buildings. Built in the 1930s, its innovative, apparently unsupported continuous ground-floor display windows remain elegantly contemporary. Refurbishment in 2008 included a new restaurant and coffee shop – Top Floor at Peter Jones.

Address Sloane Square, SW1 8EL
Nearest Tube Sloane Square
Open To The Public? Yes
Disabled accessibility Yes
Website www.johnlewis.com
Contact details 020 7730 3434

The view from the restaurant of Top Floor at Peter Jones offers an insight into a quarter of London that at street level is known to millions all over the world for its shops and museums. But this view from the triple-height picture window encapsulates what it might be like to actually live in an area of London noted for its quiet opulence. From up here, behind and above the luxurious shop fronts – invisible from here – of Gucci, Fendi and Prada in Sloane Street, you sense yourself inside another world, that of the inconspicuously moneyed residents for whom a few generations ago this part of west London was created. The residents of Knightsbridge and South

Kensington did not wish to acquire villas behind garden gates with car-littered drives as seen in certain London suburbs. Here all is cheek by jowl, jostled together in the rows of tall red-brick and terracotta mansions. This is west London as developed 160 years ago in an age utterly confident of London's imperial status in the world.

NORTH

Two essential elements turned the ancient farmlands of Brompton and Knightsbridge into the successful new residential area laid out before us. In the distance, where the tall Knightsbridge barracks stands, is Hyde Park, which by offering vast recreational open spaces with clean air in relative proximity to the West End was an immense draw to speculative builders. Trace the tree line along to the west and the shiny gold spire of the Albert Memorial in Kensington Gardens protrudes among the treetops. Proximity to the new museums and academic institutions being developed in South Kensington from the proceeds of the Great Exhibition of 1851 also assured developers that this area would be very attractive.

Just outside, in the foreground, are examples of the stepped gabled roofs in red brick with white plaster ornamentation that became the typical urban architectural style of Kensington and Knightsbridge. These homes 'wear' their history proudly with inscriptions and dates on the very apex of the highest gable. This architecture was satirically characterised as 'Pont Street Dutch' in the 1930s by cartoonist and resident Osbert Lancaster, a description which has stuck. From up here more than at street level the rooftops do look

fancifully reminiscent of the terraces lining Amsterdam's canals. They were built in an era when fires burned in the grates of upstairs nurseries and attic rooms where the household servants slept. You can almost see Bert the Sweep and Mary Poppins dancing among the tall chimney pots. Pont Street itself is identifiable by the distinctive green-grey cloche hat-shaped cupola of St Columba's Church, which stands at the western end.

The conspicuous buildings are those that began to dot the skyline in the 1960s. Mainly these are hotels – most noticeable the pale brown concrete rectangular tower of the Millennium Hotel. To its right in the distance a couple of the new glassy pavilions of London's newest and most expensive apartment complex, Number One Hyde Park, are just about visible. Parallel to

This view of red-brick and terracotta mansions is a peek into moneyed West London as it was 160 years ago.

it on the right side of the Millennium Hotel is Number One's grand old sister, the Hyde Park Hotel of 1902, now known as the Mandarin Oriental.

In the middle distance, the bold terracotta-coloured ornamented dome with a lantern tower on top identifies not a place of worship but Harrods – the mainstay of the neighbourhood since it moved here from the City in the mid 19th century. Both the dome and its adjacent tall brick chimney are invisible from street level, just a couple of the little local secrets divulged from up here.

NORTHWEST

Another such secret is the beautiful lead-coloured dome on the far left hand side of the view. That is the London Oratory of St Philip Neri – the first large Catholic church built after the Emancipation Act of 1829 and the second largest in the country. And right behind it is the open crown-shaped dome in stone that stands above the main entrance to the V&A's Edward VII building. The tall white rectangular tower with green dome is part of Imperial College, whose newest white and glass six-storey medical facility stands at the Kensington Gardens end of Exhibition Road. In the thick of all the museums, the most eye-catching collection of rooftop turrets are those belonging to the Natural History Museum. Clad in shiny grey-fawn tiles banded with white stone coursework, their elegant peaks catch the sun.

Northwards left to right: the towers of the Natural History Museum; the stone open dome above the V&A's entrance and the green cupola of Imperial College's Queen tower.

BABYLON AT DERRY AND TOMS'

WEST LONDON'S METROPOLIS FROM A SWINGING SIXTIES MECCA

Charles Derry and Joseph Toms built a retail empire on this site in the 1870s to 'serve the upper classes of South Kensington'. Their stores were responsible for putting High Street Kensington on west London's shopping map. After Derry and Toms closed in 1973, for two short years the vast department store became home to Biba – the legendary boutique that served the capital's most stylish young people in the Swinging Sixties. The Derry and Toms' Roof Garden opened in the 1930s; the garden and its famous flamingos still survive under the ownership of Richard Branson, although its fame has been eclipsed by the Babylon restaurant and bar above, loved by locals for its impressive view over west London.

Address 99 Kensington High Street, W8 5SA
Nearest Tube Kensington High Street
Open To The Public? restaurant and bar on roof terrace - booking needed
Disabled accessibility Yes
Website www.roofgardens.virgin.com
Contact details 020 7368 3993

First, from Babylon's terrace gaze immediately below to overlook parts of the original 1.5 acre roof garden – a novel idea that landed Derry and Toms' firmly among London's top social destinations for forty years. When built it boasted 500 trees and shrubs along the banks of a flowing stream with ornamental bridges where live flamingos made their home. The wild English Woodland Garden, a pretty Dutch Garden with springtime tulips and a Moorish Spanish Garden complete with arcade – considered so exotic at the time – look their best today in spring and summer.

Beyond, from seven floors up, the view highlights the relentless westward sprawl of the capital. On a clear day, gazing from the trees of Kensington Gardens in the east over to South Kensington, Earl's Court and across to the horizon hills of Wimbledon and Richmond Park, this view stretches nearly ten miles. But it looks like wall-to-wall building with barely a break.

The view from here bears out the statistics – it looks as if residential London is bursting at the seams. In the immediate foreground we overlook the densely packed terraces of South Kensington's red-brick flats with their rows of chimneys. The ceaseless, nervy sounds of human

*Then it was the roof garden of Derry &
Toms' department store...*

activity – car doors slamming,
impatient hooting, engines revving
– rise from the narrow side streets
below. This quarter is bounded by
the busy A315, better known as
Kensington High Street, and the A4 or
Cromwell Road. Further to the west,
even the planes above Heathrow
are queuing with barely 30 seconds'
landing time between them.

SOUTH

At the western corner of Babylon's
terrace, the two curved steel wings to
the south are those of the east and
west stands of Chelsea Football Club's
Stamford Bridge stadium. Fans often
gather on this terrace on match days
although there is no view of the pitch
– we are not high enough. The view is
also a reminder that Chelsea was the
first Premier League football club to

be bought by a Russian, one who has
made west London his family home.

Residential South Kensington
with Holland Park, Hyde Park and
Heathrow nearby has traditionally
seemed more exotic and wealthy
than other parts of London, with
a high concentration of families
coming from abroad to take up
temporary residence. Close to main
roads, many of the larger, more
modern buildings seen from up here
are hotels and apartment blocks
rather than offices. Commercially
speaking, we overlook an area that
has come to prominence as home
to exhibitions and entertainment.
A little to the right, Earl's Court Two
with its barrel-shaped glass roof and
red iron tracery spans the District
Line tracks and adjoins the taller
white concrete building behind
called Earl's Court One. When built
in 1937 it was the largest reinforced
concrete structure in Europe. Slightly
to the west and north, about half
a mile away, another barrel-shaped
glass entrance stands out with a
plain brick building behind. That is
Olympia, which in conjunction with
Earl's Court provides London's two
best-known international exhibition
centres, attracting millions of visitors
into the capital each year.

EAST

Business exhibitions began with
Prince Albert's Great Exhibition
of 1851, featuring new industrial
products from all corners of the

world. Next time you pass the Albert Memorial, look for the catalogue in the Prince's golden right hand. From Babylon's terrace the Memorial's gothic golden-edged roof and spire are visible to the extreme left, rising above the trees of Kensington Gardens with the Park Lane Hilton tower just behind it.

The near skyline in this direction is indeed a homage to the age of Prince Albert and Queen Victoria. The shallow three-layered glass dome of the Albert Hall is visible in unusual detail between the Shard and the pyramid roof of Canary Wharf to the left and the topmost pinnacles of the Victoria Tower, the sovereign's entrance to the Houses of Parliament, on its right. Two more recent buildings interrupt the Victorian roofscape: the black and white Strata tower, standing in profile from here, looks like a pen's quill as it cosies up to Westminster Cathedral's campanile, much closer to us, the latter appearing to rival in shape and height the 287ft white Portland stone Queen's Tower of Imperial College with its green domed roof. The grey slate dome just behind this tops the London Oratory of St Philip Neri, while an elegant crown-shaped open dome immediately to the right of that is the very top of the grand entrance to the Edward VII wing of the V&A. An array of turrets in stone, terracotta, brick and copper mark Alfred Waterhouse's palatial Natural History Museum next door.

...Now it is the Kensington Roof Gardens of Richard Branson's Babylon nightclub. The flamingos have remained.

RICHMOND HILL

AN EXCLUSIVE ARCADIA NEAR THE HEART OF LONDON

To the west of Richmond Park, on a hill above the thoroughfare of historic Richmond itself, is a view down to the Thames more frequently painted and eulogised in poem and song than any other in London. The Royal Borough of Richmond was absorbed into London in 1890, prior to which it was part of Surrey. Residents continue to address the preservation of this view since an Act of Parliament in 1902 gave it legal protection. They know the Hill and its view has been one of the reasons why Richmond attracts some of London's wealthiest citizens to settle here.

Address Richmond Hill, TW10
Nearest Tube Richmond
Open To The Public? Yes
Disabled accessibility Steep hill

A row of lovely houses called Downe Terrace stands on the top of Richmond Hill. With the open fields of Richmond Park to the south and the town of Richmond and its former royal palace to its north, the hill has been a spot where thousands have stopped to gaze down at the beautiful rolling meadows leading to the Thames far below. On a summer evening, with cows and pleasure boats in sight, it seems strange to call this a London skyline.

It is awe-inspiring for one major reason: barely tampered with in the past few hundred years, it can boast of remaining the most rural of all London's skyline views. There are not many places in London from which the river is visible at this height. Views of the Thames from central London can be equally beautiful but never show a 'benign' river without crowds, the tide, the currents, or with the green we see here. On the next curve upriver is Teddington Lock, beyond which the Thames is no longer tidal.

SOUTHWEST

The view overlooks one of the many steep curves of the tortuous Thames upstream from central London. Midway between its banks is a wooded island – named Glover's Island after a former owner – with one or two boats tethered close to it. Following the sweep of the waters on this side of its banks sits historic Ham House, peeping out from between the trees. Just visible in Marble Hill Park on the opposite bank is Marble Hill House. To top it all off, on a clear day even Windsor Castle comes into the picture.

At first glance this view defines quintessential England's green and pleasant land: a lyrical curl of the river through lush meadows with an island, an aristocratic home or two peeping through the trees to left and right, and, visible on the left at the southern end of Downe Terrace, the jolly Roebuck pub up on the Hill itself – all idealised, frozen in aspic, with very little connection to metropolitan London.

But look again, because this skyline defines London's gaping contrasts of 'us and them'. Of the thousands coming to marvel at the timeless beauty of the Thames, how many could ever afford to live here? The endless stream of planes above preparing to land at concealed Heathrow provides a constant reminder of the capital's international importance. And the prominence of London's most important rugby football venue rises in all its futuristic glory above the trees to the west in Twickenham. After only a moment's gazing, the lack of audible birdsong despite the rural nature of this view is another reminder that this is London.

The cantilevered edifice of Twickenham rugby stadium beyond the verdant calm of Richmond Hill.

The A307 Petersham to Richmond Road just below actually divides the viewer from the Thames meadows in the distance, but fortunately it is camouflaged well enough by trees, even in winter, not to disrupt the Arcadian illusion. Also, fortunately, there is a little tunnel under the road that leads from the Buccleuch Terrace gardens below to the river's edge and the Petersham Meadows.

NORTH

Along the gravel terrace at the top of the hill just a few steps to the north, looking down through the landscaped Victorian Terrace Gardens to the river in that direction there is a glimpse of the stonework of Richmond Bridge, and further along the river path is the iron railway bridge that crosses the Thames to Twickenham. It is possible to make out, peeping

The 'keyhole' view of St Paul's from Richmond Park's Pembroke Lodge.

from the trees beside this bridge, the pale beige Palladian villa Asgill House, built in 1711, that stands on the edge of Richmond's other park, Old Deer Park – now a sports ground and golf course.

NORTHEAST

Close by this viewpoint, just through Richmond Gate into Richmond Park, a raised area known as King Henry VIII's Mound offers another protected view. A linear view rather than a skyline as such, and not nearly so well known as the one from Richmond Hill, it nevertheless presents an uninterrupted 'keyhole' vista across ten miles, focused uniquely on the lantern, dome and peristyle of St Paul's Cathedral. Created in the early 18th century, at the time St Paul's was completed, this view has been framed by the planting of an avenue of trees and foliage as the crow flies to the City. Man-managed ever since – today by City Hall – its aperture can vary according to the seasons and the amount of regular pruning carried out.

Like looking through an early pinhole camera, the light shines on the Cathedral showing a huge expanse of sky behind and above. It is scarcely believable that such a view is not a two-dimensional picture at the end of a tunnel. To the left, a sliver of the recently completed Broadgate Tower has managed to insinuate itself into the vista, lending a slightly more 3D quality to the view.

HORSENDEN HILL

FIVE COUNTIES FROM A REMNANT OF RURAL WEST LONDON

Rising 275ft above sea level, Horsenden Hill – roughly 14 miles from Charing Cross and marking the western extremity of metropolitan London – is one of four ancient conservation sites in the borough of Ealing. Several field ponds near the hill have been restored and now support various amphibian populations including the specially protected great crested newt. The site also includes two golf courses. Since 2011 a government-backed scheme has provided funding for management of this site that includes hay cutting, grazing and maintenance of reed beds.

Address Horsenden Lane North, UB6
Nearest Tube Sudbury Town
Disabled accessibility Some rough terrain

Wild woodland paths lead up to the cleared hilltop of Horsenden Hill, from where a skyline to the north, west and east provides views of no less than five counties. Buckinghamshire, Berkshire, Hertfordshire, Middlesex and Surrey can all be seen from here. It is an excellent and largely unsung spot from which to stake out rural walks close to central London. Not only can the gamut of the capital's most famous high-rises be seen from here; from the flat clearance on the top of the hill, the view is a peep into outer London's immediate industrial past.

It is recommended to stick to the main paths alongside ancient hedges, woodland and pasture on the way up to the top, where Neolithic and Iron Age farming remains have been excavated. Horsenden Hill itself is at the southwest of the well-researched Barnet Plateau Natural Landscape Area – an arc around west London identified by surviving patches of medieval field and farmland.

SOUTHWEST

Downhill on the western side, the rugby posts below lie on fields that were used for growing wheat and vegetables during the Second World War and remained in cultivation until about 1950. In the distance the tall bright blue Southall water tower, close to the banks of the River Yeading and the Grand Union Canal, acts as a convenient orientation point. In the middle distance in front of it and to the left sits the Royal Mail's Greenford Mail Centre, and adjacent is a swathe of flat silver-grey factory roofs that belong to Greenford Green Industrial

Park. The roofs of IBM's Global Technology Services building give the foreground a strong industrial flavour. The Grand Union Canal comes flowing eastwards between the IBM building and Horsenden Lane North, which is the road running alongside the foot of the hill.

Southwards beyond South Greenford and Perivale Park, the North Downs on the Surrey border make up the skyline on the horizon to the extreme left. Below us, hidden by trees, is the Great Western Road (A40), its traffic sounds quite prominent.

WEST

Follow the skyline to the right and the horizon becomes Egham, Virginia Water and Windsor Great Park in Berkshire. In the middle distance to the right, in Greenford, a mix of rooftops are interspersed with those of well-known manufacturing names like pharmaceutical giant Glaxo on the Greenford Road, which established its headquarters here as Beechams before the Second World War. The original lab survives with the newer laboratories next door. Other once famous names along this road like J. Lyons and Sandersons are long gone. Beyond the Greenford Road is a landmark 1960s block built where, when this was Middlesex, the Northolt Race Course once stood. Just to the left on a parallel sightline is Northolt RAF Aerodrome, bordered by the A40 but only identifiable from here if a plane is landing or taking off.

NORTH

Looking across from northwest to northeast, the Chiltern Hills of Buckinghamshire form the skyline. In the middle distance beyond a

Northwest from Horsenden Hill towards Ruislip Woods. Allen Court is the tall block to the left.

Wembley Stadium appears breathtakingly close to the east.

sea of red suburban roofs we catch a glimpse of the treetops of Ruislip Woods about eight miles away; a popular destination for London ramblers, these 726 acres of natural woodland in the London Borough of Hillingdon are within a few metres of an underground station.

Standing out from the pastoral skyline on this northerly view is the ten-storey residential Allen Court – the only tall building for miles around, providing a handy reference point. To the left of it on the horizon are the old market towns of Hemel Hempstead and Watford in Hertfordshire. To the right is a fine view of Harrow on the Hill, with the tall spire of St Mary's Church just discernible between the trees. To the right of that and in the distance is Bentley Priory in Stanmore, Middlesex, headquarters of RAF Fighter Command during the

Battle of Britain and now becoming a much-visited scientific interest and nature reserve site of 163 acres. Continue scanning the horizon to the right and the most distant hill easily visible is Mill Hill in the London Borough of Barnet.

EAST

Horsenden Hill golf course adjoins the crest of the hill. Looking down the fairway, the urban complex of Wembley Stadium with its defining arch appears breathtakingly close. Walking around the hilltop to face due east, it is possible to catch through the trees a stunning linear skyline view of the cluster of buildings and monuments that define the capital today – among them the Gherkin, Broadgate Tower, Tower 42 and Heron Tower in the City, and Number One Canada Square, Barclays and Citigroup in Canary Wharf.

ALEXANDRA PALACE

AN 'ALL OR NOTHING' VIEW ACROSS SOUTH LONDON

High on a hill above north London, Alexandra Palace opened as an exhibition centre in 1875. Although named after the then Princess of Wales, later the wife of Edward VII, it was never a royal residence, but was purpose-built to provide a large hall, a concert room, offices, a reading room and a theatre. Ally Pally (its local nickname) has since been used as a barracks for First World War Belgian refugees and Second World War German prisoners, as BBC television studios and as a venue for concerts and horse and dog shows. Today the grand conservatory hall on the west, the Palm Court, provides an event space and restaurants while indoor sports facilities take up the east side conservatory. Outside is the landmark transmitter from which, on 2 November 1936, the world's first regular public television service was broadcast by the BBC. The updated radio tower is still in use.

Address Alexandra Palace Way, N22 7AY
Nearest Tube Alexandra Park National Rail
Open To The Public? Yes
Disabled accessibility Yes
Website www.alexandrapalace.com
Contact details 020 8365 2121

From the Palace forecourt, known as South Terrace, the view is stunning in its scale and depth. This is a perfect viewpoint from which to get the measure of the skyline across northeast and southeast London and the City. It is a mesmerising 'all or nothing' view: in summer with the sun high, in perfect light, the viewing radius to the east and south covers a clear 25 miles, but one hill about a mile away obscures the sightline from here to central London. Frustratingly, to the west, the view is abruptly halted by Muswell Hill, on which Alexandra Palace itself stands, and the other nearby north London hills.

EAST

Walking in 'panoramic fashion' from the left or east side of South Terrace, the local landmarks of Wood Green and Hornsey – redbrick Shopping City, the Great Northern Railway tracks and brown gas tanks – dominate the view. A striking new white and yellow housing estate called New River Village marks the banks of the culverted New River, an early 17th-century man-made channel designed to bring fresh Hertfordshire river water to the City of London. At this point on its course from Chadwell to Sadler's Wells, the New River feeds the treatment reservoirs visible on

The eastern prospect, with Wood Green's red-brick Shopping City in front of the pale brick towers and blocks of Tottenham's Broadwater Farm Estate.

the eastern extremity of Alexandra Park. Further to the west the view pans across South Tottenham with the towers of Broadwater Farm estate close to the smoking factory chimneys of Walthamstow, and beyond to Ilford and the hills of Essex.

SOUTHEAST

Southwards of here, there is a great overview of the Olympic Park. The stadium, Anish Kapoor's Orbit sculpture and the white 'flat pack' basketball arena stand out brightly. The hubs of the Athletes' Village peep out behind the basketball arena, with the Pringle-shaped velodrome to the left of the park and the wings of the aquatic centre to the right. South of the Olympic Park the skyline of Stratford High Street's bold new residential tower blocks emphasises

the knock-on development effects of London's successful bid for the 2012 Games. Beyond, the east London skyline south of the river is dominated by the beautiful curve of Shooters Hill. To the right, the towers of Canary Wharf interrupt the curve; from this distance, they look in winter like ghostly apparitions in the grey light.

An unusual geographic blip in tree-lined suburbia appears closer to the foreground. Look below the forecourt and Alexandra Park rolls steeply away to an area called Hornsey Vale. Beyond, the land rises to the east–west ridgeline of Crouch Hill. An amusing pattern of six parallel roads, each lined with rows of houses, climb to the top looking like snowless ski jumps. From up here Crouch Hill itself obscures acres of London to the south like Holloway, Highbury and Islington; the next tall skyline structures that appear beyond it are the tops of those identifying the City of London six and a half miles away. The most prominent cluster contains the Heron Tower, Tower 42, the highest part of the Willis Building and the Gherkin, along with a new member: the core of the so-called Walkie Talkie tower, 20 Fenchurch Street.

SOUTH

From the City towers it is a small step to the right where the ubiquitous Shard looms. Then suddenly the dome of St Paul's lurks between the trees of Alexandra Park and next to it the Strata south of the Thames stands in solitude, its silhouette looking like an old-fashioned electric razor. Beyond, the Crystal Palace and Croydon transmitters line up on the horizon.

As you walk along to the right (or west) side of South Terrace, the

hills of north London cut off central London landmarks. The Thames at Waterloo is signified by a view of the very top of the Shell Centre – that rectangular white stone block with a distinctive 'shrunken' top floor and shallow canopy-style pointed roof – and a partial, ellipsoidal view of the London Eye.

SOUTHWEST

A view of the topmost part of Centre Point signals the 'end' of the West End; further west, local neighbourhood hill views feature as Highgate and Queen's Wood obscure London beyond. The prominent white tower residential block is Avenue Heights in front of Hornsey Lane, a hill on which low-rise blocks of flats march up to meet Highgate Hill and the two green domes of St Joseph's Church. On top of Highgate Hill the spire of St Michael's Church and a massive transmitter mark the skyline.

The southeastern prospect, with Crouch Hill ridge fronting the distant towers of Canary Wharf.

PARLIAMENT HILL

THE CITIES OF LONDON AND WESTMINSTER FROM THE CAPITAL'S GREENEST SPACE

Hampstead Heath, less than four miles north of Trafalgar Square, is one of London's most popular open spaces. Its 790-acre expanse of beautiful countryside is shared between two London boroughs – Camden and Barnet. The magic of Hampstead Heath lies not only in its being a haven rich in wildlife and offering extensive sports and recreational facilities, but also in its proximity and accessibility to millions of people. From 1829 a protracted struggle by local people that ended in an Act of Parliament in 1871 has kept Hampstead Heath protected from developers. There is no similar breadth of countryside left within central London today that still links so completely with its countryside origins.

Address Parliament Hill, NW3
Nearest Tube Hampstead Heath
Overground National Rail
Disabled accessibility Steep hill

Parliament Hill on Hampstead Heath is said by some to have got its name from having been the site from where Guy Fawkes and his fellow conspirators were hoping to watch the destruction of the Houses of Parliament on 5 November 1605. Others say it comes from a period about 40 years after Guy Fawkes' abortive coup when it became a point of defence for troops loyal to Parliament during the English Civil War. But either reason would be implausible today. Spotting the Palace of Westminster as rebuilt in 1860, even with the massive Clock Tower containing Big Ben, is almost impossible. Only the highest point of the Victoria Tower is visible now.

SOUTH

On a sunny autumn morning the view south from the apex of the hill – a stainless steel plaque, placed here by Camden Council in 1984, marks the spot – is shrouded in mist, making London appear like a phantom city in shades of grey. The panoramic east–west scale of this view is what makes it so dramatically special. There cannot be many vantage points from which the two cities of London and Westminster can be viewed side by side on equal terms from the same distant spot.

At the foot of the hill lie the athletics track and the outdoor pool known as the Lido. The first construction that comes into view is the controversial

Gospel Oak's athletics track is below, with the City beyond.

1970s white tower by Lismore Circus, in Gospel Oak. It will soon lose its prominence as the new high-rises of 67 acres of regeneration of King's Cross Central, shoehorned into the neglected former railway lands to the north of King's Cross and St Pancras, take shape. Further away to the west, there is a good view of the campanile of Westminster Cathedral and Westminster City Hall, both along Victoria Street.

SOUTHEAST

The furthest views to the southeast from here include Canary Wharf's shapely crop of towers, but the old City's cluster, closer in proximity, is more distinct. The West End views to the right of the City are barely distinguishable except for the icon of Swinging Sixties London, the BT Tower, standing in splendid isolation in Fitzrovia and looking all the more remarkable at dusk when its silhouette is lit up in purple, blue and pink. The green glazed Euston Tower is the only other prominent landmark.

It is undeniable that even while still under construction, the Shard has become the landmark attraction from the Hill. Even St Paul's, sitting right in front of it, has begun to look like a mere foil – something the London planners will no doubt eventually realise and come to regret. Some of the bigger species of trees on Parliament Hill are so tall now they obscure almost all the more local landmarks etched in the stainless steel plan placed on the crest. Sadly, developers – with the help of nature – have transformed Parliament Hill from a great lookout over London into what is becoming known to locals by its nickname, Kite Hill.

NORTHEAST

Turning away from central London in the south to face northeast, where the kite flyers race around the green valley that leads down to Highgate Ponds, the north London landscape has become a more interesting view. Beyond this wide expanse of hilly open green, the clear outline of Highgate Hill slopes up from the dark brown Archway Tower and past the turrets of the Whittington Hospital. Halfway up is the bright green copper dome of St Joseph's Church, or Holy Joe's as it is known locally.

Close to the peak of Highgate West Hill nestles Witanhurst – reputedly London's second largest private home after Buckingham Palace. Originally built in the 18th century, Witanhurst has more recently been at the heart of a real estate mystery story as successive owners have failed to establish plans for its renovation; as a result, the 65-bedroom mansion, rebuilt early in the 20th century by soap magnate Arthur Crosfield, and with a fantastic and somewhat scandalous history, has fallen into increasingly expensive disrepair. At this distance its brick façade, punctuated by white columns and topped off with a steep red-tiled roof, looks like the perfect setting for an urban Downton Abbey-style blockbuster romance.

Lower down the slopes that face Parliament Hill, in high contrast to Witanhurst is a brutalist concrete structure with a massive white satellite dish hanging off the elevation facing the Heath. How it evaded the planners' condemnation is explained by the fact that it is the headquarters of the Russian Trade Legation, set up here during the Cold War to be near the grave of Karl Marx in Highgate Cemetery.

Who could resist drawing up their bike to take in London laid out beneath?

PRIMROSE HILL

A CONDENSED VISION OF MODERN LONDON

There are no flowers today, but Primrose Hill on the north side of Regent's Park retains the name as a wistful reminder of its ancient rural aspect, when each year its sides were covered with early spring blooms. Once owned by Eton College, the 200ft high hill and the surrounding land are now a public thoroughfare. Close to central London but with an atmosphere of calm apparent in the surrounding streets of pastel Victorian villas, Primrose Hill also happens to be one of London's most important sightlines; dozens of architectural plans for central London have been restrained for interfering with this popular, historic view.

Address Near Prince Albert Road, NW8 7LU
Nearest Tube Camden Town
Disabled accessibility Steep hill

The top of Primrose Hill has been gravelled over recently and made into a viewpoint, complete with a stone surround and seats. About 150 years ago the view due south would have been limited to the rebuilt Palace of Westminster with its three towers, the dome and bell towers of St Paul's Cathedral and, to the east and much closer, the magnificent single-span trainshed, designed by William Barlow, of St Pancras Station. Today it's worth taking a seat, because this view is a condensed version of modern London, one that requires deciphering.

SOUTHEAST

Facing south, London's buildings billow out towards the horizon with no space in between. To pinpoint some landmarks, first look east to the long, low-rise 1960s Market Estate on York Way, standing out on a low hill. Its length is punctuated behind by the old Caledonian Market's clock tower (still known locally as the Ebonite Tower), which would have been very prominent 150 years ago when it marked the capital's largest live animal market. More prominent today are the cranes framing skeletons of new housing blocks on the northern part of the King's Cross Central site. Pull your gaze in closer to distinguish the span of St Pancras' single-span glass trainshed, sitting before the Gothic fairy towers of the reopened station's Renaissance Hotel.

From this height east London's landmarks, like the new extension of the Royal London Hospital with its rooftop helipad, look as if they stand alongside the giants of Canary Wharf. Perspective pulls all the City's newest additions, like the Heron Tower, Gherkin and Willis Building, closely together; the Barbican's towers rub shoulders with Tower 42 behind. Closer to the foot of Primrose Hill, three dominant creamy-brown towers line the start of Hampstead Road. They stand on the opposite side of the road from the 1830s east portal of the Primrose Hill Railway Tunnel, invisible from this height.

SOUTH

Looking due south, straight ahead, the line of Euston Road is easy to follow with the deep green glass of Euston Station and the paler green and white new Wellcome Building

and adjacent new University College Hospital block and tower. Directly behind, the ubiquitous Shard, and Guy's Hospital behind that, indicate the south side of London Bridge, as does the deep brown tower of Tate Modern. It is just possible to make out the citrus-coloured façades of Central St Giles next to Centre Point; its apparent neighbour, the Strata, is a couple of miles away in Elephant and Castle.

Beyond the Palace of Westminster's towers, the spire of St George's Church on the south side of the Thames in Southwark and unidentified buildings surrounding it seem much less jumbled than in the rest of London. With no bridges or river visible from this angle, the spire is the only indication as to where the Thames might be flowing. The Shell Centre

One of the finest picnic spots anywhere in London.

The three towers of the Ampthill Square Estate by Hampstead Road with the Gherkin behind and St Paul's to the right.

at Waterloo on the south bank is the backdrop to the BT Tower, which itself forms the backdrop to the new Regent's Place development, just north of Portland Street Station. John Nash's white Palladian villas guide our eyes into Regent's Park, at the foot of the south side of Primrose Hill, but the only identifiable features of the Zoological Gardens inside the Park itself are the tent-like 1960s Snowdon Aviary and the brown stepped 'mountain' for the antelopes behind.

Still looking south, but beyond the cupola of St Marylebone Church in the middle distance, we can make out the dome of Westminster Cathedral's polychrome brick bell tower, the Millbank Tower behind and the new glassy retail/residential developments of Victoria close to its station. Those grey tiled turrets are the French Renaissance revival rooftops of Grosvenor Gardens and Grosvenor Road, just about distinguishable as you gaze towards the tallest and most distinct modern tower building in the view, Knightsbridge Barracks.

Even more distinct is the copper-green cupola and belfry of the Queen's Tower in South Kensington, the only focal point of sprawling Imperial College visible from Parliament Hill.

SOUTHWEST

Closer to home, to the west, the post-Second World War development of London's suburbs just north of the West End can be deciphered. Starting with Adelaide Road in Chalk Farm, the sixties residential tower blocks built alongside the railway tracks as they briefly emerge from the west portal of Primrose Hill Tunnel are nearest and clearly visible. Further west it is possible to trace the spread of tall 1960s residential estates along Adelaide Road at Swiss Cottage and down to Carlton Vale. Turning your back on the capital's more scenic landmarks, the two distinctive adjoining blocks of Trellick Tower close to Portobello Road suddenly come into focus.

THE NEW LONDON ARCHITECTURE MODEL

LONDON'S FUTURE IN MINIATURE

Enter the Building Centre on Store Street and a perfect 1:1500 scale model of London is presented on the ground floor. It attracts the first-time visitor with a magnetic power. New London Architecture (NLA) was founded here in 2005 by a partnership between Wordsearch, an international marketing and property company, and model makers Pipers. Together they created this model of London based on the areas where the most building activity takes place. Corresponding to the Ordnance Survey grid, it is updated frequently to provide everyone from students to influential architects and planners with a basis for discussion of London's built environment.

Address 26 Store Street, WC1E 7BT
Nearest Tube Goodge Street
Open To The Public? Mon-Fri 9:30am-6:00pm, Sat 10:00am-5:00pm
Disabled accessibility Yes
Website www.newlondonarchitecture.org
Contact details 020 7636 4044

As we pore over the model that illustrates just a fraction of Greater London from Paddington to the Royal Docks and from King's Cross to Battersea, it becomes a powerful tool in modifying our sense of space. It isolates then shrinks our sense of our actual size, enabling us to imagine it is possible to enter its scale. At the same time it expands the mind, allowing it to absorb a wealth of three-dimensional detail. It is mesmerising. Time evaporates. Should it have a health warning?

If ever proof were needed, this model testifies to London as a city with one of the world's largest and most complex skylines. Almost 2000 years in the making, it is evident from its layout that London is a fluid growth of villages linked to each other around the nucleus of the City and Westminster. The model illustrates clearly how the Thames, furrowing through a landmass on its way to the sea, left a jigsaw of peninsulas north and south that a toddler could put together. The river's route has been made more complex in the east by a network of man-made channels (some since virtually erased by Docklands regeneration projects; the connections between St Katherine's Dock, via the London Dock, to Tobacco Dock and the Shadwell Basin are all but filled in today) sliced through the land to accommodate river commerce – the

A view of the Thames's western reaches as they will be with a regenerated Vauxhall in the foreground.

reason for London's existence since Roman times.

The model was built with a unique legend that aids comprehension enormously. It is predominantly grey – the colour signifying buildings that exist in London as it is now. An unexpected result is that it provokes awareness of how fast time flies and how in its trail so many controversies are buried. The Gherkin, finished in 2004, is in grey. Was it that long ago? The white buildings are works in progress or recently completed, or for which planning approval has been gained. Strips of green, orange, blue, red and black weaving in and out of London's chaotic grid identify various types of existing and planned transport networks; looking down at the model, they clearly indicate where the key to those developing white bits lies.

Everything is to scale and shape. White buildings tend to be mostly towers, some in huge clusters that

build on earlier successes – as we see in the heart of the City, for example, as well as in new East India and around the Stratford Olympic Park area. But others, like the triple triangular cluster that stands around the Paddington Basin or the double crystal of Siemens' urban sustainability centre on the Royal Victoria Dock, reflect in miniature how bold new architectural schemes are leading the way in places where no skyline buildings have ever previously existed.

No less impressive are the relatively tiny, isolated architectural 'infills' of the West End, like Eric Parry's recent Savile Row rebuild, whose interesting forms bravely punctuate the traditional, reflecting the strict planning constraints enforced in certain central London areas.

According to the model, Nine Elms between Vauxhall and Battersea Power Station appears to be set to emerge as a whole new area of

How the City will look when all its planned new skyscrapers have been built.

post-Olympic London. Apart from a new US Embassy planned to absorb five acres, the area's regeneration will incorporate high- and medium-rise residential and office blocks and towers, a primary school and recreation areas. A linear public park linking the Covent Garden Market side at the Vauxhall (east) end to the restored and rebuilt Battersea Power Station complex in the west is a route equal in length to Oxford Street. Not even started yet but also modelled in white is the monumental building project that will take up an entire peninsula between Canning Town and Leamouth. Such optimism is reassuring.

This view of the London skyline in miniature invokes purely the positive. At a time of precarious financial conditions that threaten not a few schemes, London needs a model to follow and keep its aspirations for the future alive.

A skyline view of London from ground level.

HEIGHTS AT ST GEORGE'S HOTEL

AN UNSUNG VENUE FROM WHICH TO WATCH THE WEST END GO BY

In the heart of west London, minutes from Oxford Street to the south and Regent's Park to the north, the St George's Hotel, built in the 1960s, thrives next to its grander and better known neighbour the Langham. For all its history – home to visiting celebrities like Mark Twain, Toscanini and Dvorak, as well as exiled royals such as Haile Selassie and Napoleon III – the Langham's restaurant cannot compete for views with the 15th-floor bar and dining room of St George's, The Heights. It must be the best unsung restaurant in London from which to watch the world go by.

Address Regent Street, W1B 2QS
Nearest Tube Oxford Circus
Open To The Public? For drinks and dining
Disabled accessibility Yes
Website www.stgeorgeshotel.com
Contact details 020 7580 0111

WEST

At a window table facing west, the Heights Restaurant is low enough to provide a fairly intimate view of West End life below, yet high enough for a raking glance all the way across west London's relatively low-rise skyline. The bulky grey brick 19th-century Langham Hotel sits on the other side of the road where a grand mansion called Foley House once stood. Its owner, Lord Foley, forced John Nash, the Prince Regent's architect, to increase the width of his processional route to Regent's Park so as not to obscure the skyline view from his windows of Hampstead and Highgate. There is an excellent view of the Langham's architectural features: its grand domed roof, a domed faux bell tower, a huge double-height bow window over Regent Street and an ornamental frieze encircling the building just below the roof, all invisible from street level.

So close you may not even notice it at first is the fluted Portland stone spire of All Souls Church, suddenly appearing slightly below window level as it shoots upwards from a circular podium surrounded by Corinthian columns. This church with its unusual spire, designed by Nash to mask the crick in his route, was bitterly criticised, the 19th-century political cartoonist George

Cruickshank depicting the architect being pierced up his backside by his own creation.

Curves and spires seem to echo each other across the rooftops. The curve of All Souls' porticoed entrance is repeated in the bow of the grand window of the Langham opposite and in the broad sweeping curve of Val Myers' 1931 Broadcasting House on the other side. An adjacent extension to the BBC, recently completed by architects MacCormick Jamieson Pritchard, repeats the sweep and curve. On the roof of the BBC two transmission towers on different levels echo in shape the spire of All Souls.

NORTHWEST

In the middle distance to the north, the golden statues around the cupola of St Marylebone Church stand out against the green trees and exotic white domed roofs of Nash's Regent's Park Terraces. Just behind sits the massive golden dome of the Central London Mosque. The Wembley arch behind it pokes up from the blue-green horizon shrouded in blue-grey mist like a classical ruin in the far distance of a Claude Lorraine landscape.

Back to the middle distance, we can see the white stone clock tower of Abbey House at 219-29 Baker Street (encompassing no. 221b, the address of Sherlock Holmes, which would have been on the site before it), part

of a residential block redeveloped in 2008. To the south the terracotta clock tower of Marylebone Station appears to stand next door to the terracotta and glass curves of the new builds at Paddington Basin.

SOUTH

Looking south, to the immediate left the 'T'-shaped glass tower of the London College of Fashion dwarfs its white Portland stone neighbour John Lewis, with six rooftop logo-clad flagstaffs hanging over its Cavendish Square façade. Directly behind, the vast red-brick fortress with corner turrets like a 1930s version of an Italian basilica is the Grosvenor House Hotel complex between Park Lane and Park Street, with Knightsbridge

Nash's All Souls Church with Broadcasting House behind, including its new rear extension.

Looking north over Marylebone to the BT Tower and Euston Tower beyond.

Barracks sticking up right behind it. Between the two extreme towers of Grosvenor House on the left, the stone-buttressed crown of the Edward VII Wing of the V&A in South Kensington appears. To the right of the barracks is the green copper cupola of the white stone Queen's Tower of Imperial College. Just a little to the right is an unusual sight of the Royal Albert Hall's vast cupola; its base invisible, it looks more like a UFO. Even rarer is a glimpse to the right of the top of Albert's Memorial in profile.

Closer to home on the right, two red cranes mark Oxford Street's newest single whole-block development, rising opposite Selfridges like a giant humpback glass bridge. On a clear day the four towers of Battersea Power Station form the skyline, looking from this angle like backing formation dancers for their

neighbouring giant blue water tower to the right and Millbank Tower to the left.

EAST

From the window on the opposite (bar) side of the Heights restaurant, east London's giant new signature buildings establish themselves along the curve of the Thames – itself only identifiable by the turrets of Tower Bridge. To the right the silhouette of the Shard in the far distance brings into focus before it the splay-footed spire, with contrasting bands of stone and charcoal-grey brick and an ornate wrought-iron cross on top, of All Saints Church, Margaret Street.

On the same sightline to the left the BT Tower dominates like a bastion on the northeast edge of Marylebone's residential grid, almost leaning on top of University College Hospital's new green and white complex. London University's stolid stone Senate House dominates low-rise Bloomsbury with just a corner of the British Museum's green glass roof appearing from behind a block of flats. Centre Point is a useful orientating landmark, but the lime green and orange splashes of the Central St Giles development next door are far more prominent. In the distance among the high-density jumble of houses the clock tower of the former Caledonian Market looks far more impressive from here than it does close up, rivalling the restored fairy towers and spires of St Pancras visible just beyond.

CLOSED TO THE PUBLIC

NUMBER ONE CANADA SQUARE

OLD EAST LONDON FROM THE HEART OF THE NEW

Briefly the tallest building in Europe when completed in 1991, Number One Canada Square still symbolises the international financial muscle at the heart of Canary Wharf. The 38 lifts in the 50-storey building are dedicated to sections of its height, so it takes barely 45 seconds to reach the 45th floor. Aeroplanes ascending from City Airport, just a mile or so away, wing by the north window – a reminder why the building's pyramid roof was topped by its permanently flashing light.

Address Canada Square, E1H 5AB
Nearest Tube Canary Wharf

The view from this London icon spotlights what was happening to the rest of east London while regeneration revolutionised the Docklands area in the 1980s and 1990s. From One Canada Square's north-facing window, non-riverside Limehouse, Poplar and Blackwall between two white stone churches (St Anne's to the west and All Saints to the east) appear barely touched. From up here they are not simply 771ft down – they are a world away.

NORTHWEST

To the left, in Canary Wharf itself the vast quadrangle of the old Cannon Workshops is revealed from the north window, standing adjacent to a row of original warehouses. The only remnants of the late 17th-century West India Quay, they now house the Docklands Museum.

Across the busy Aspen Way that binds the north side of Canary Wharf, the Docklands Light Railway trundles off north and east. Through the heart of Poplar, surviving fragments of the Lansbury Estate, built in 1951 for the Festival of Britain, are evident along the sparse streets immediately north of East India Dock Road, whose names like Nankin and Pekin evoke the original Chinatown of docklands London.

Alongside a few Victorian terraced streets and the copper-domed St Mary and St Joseph's church on Canton Street, there is a strong hint even from this height of a resilient community. With small parks, small gardens and small schools, it endures within spitting distance of Canary Wharf's behemoth futuristic vision.

Poplar today is a triangle defined by Aspen Way to the south, the Limehouse Cut to the west and the A12 Blackwall Tunnel Northern Approach, finished in 1972, to the east. The A12 Approach, which cuts across the skyline to the right, was built almost simultaneously with Westway in west London, which similarly cut a swathe through a local community. Poplar even has its own Erno Goldfinger-designed 1960s concrete residential block, the Balfron Tower – prototype of the Trellick Tower in Westbourne Grove. Sandwiched between St Leonards Road and the A12 close to its junction with East India Dock Road, the building's brown-grey two-part profile actually overlooks the six-lane Blackwall Tunnel Approach.

Opposite the east-facing side of All Saints Church is a good view of the two ten-storey concrete blocks of the Robin Hood Gardens estate, also built in 1972, an oasis surrounded on all sides by ever bigger new road junctions and now earmarked for demolition.

Just to the northeast where the tributaries of the River Lee gather into Bow Creek, the low factory and depot roofs and a rusting gasholder testify to east London's lingering industrial nature. Here the old communities of St Leonards and Bromley by Bow, victims of the A12, are at last beginning to

Eastwards over the Dome and past London City Airport to the left and all the way to the oil refineries of the Thames Estuary.

pick themselves up again thanks to Olympic regeneration.

The Olympic Park beyond may itself look a disparate hodgepodge of venues. But by 2013 it will re-emerge as east London's new park, dwarfing mile-long Mile End Park seen to the west with Mile End Stadium marking its southern side. A mass of trees to the north indicates where it meets Victoria Park – not to be confused with a smaller cluster marking Tower Hamlets Cemetery.

WEST

From the west-facing windows, the soft 'S' curve of the Thames guides the eye across the unfolding drama of central London, compressing its detail. The Wembley Arch appears almost in the centre of this 28-mile conurbation – if that smoking chimney on the horizon is indeed in Slough. In between, a mass of skyline icons jostle for attention on the north bank. The giant Shard stands solitary on the south bank, quietly confident it has surpassed in height the challenge of Number One Canada Square.

SOUTH

Directly below, there is a pleasing symmetry to Canary Wharf's layout. At the east end, Churchill Place links Canada Square to Cartier Circus with its bronze stelae sculpture. At the opposite end, Westferry Circus at the Thames edge links to West India Avenue and Cabot Square with its computer-controlled fountains.

Number One Canada Square

North over the Olympic Park, with the Stadium on the right.

Further south, the surviving Inner and Outer Millwall Docks forming the core of the Isle of Dogs are visible but the view is otherwise largely obscured by the twin JP Morgan Towers and Pan Peninsula on the South Quay.

On London's south side, surrounded by much lower-rise housing estates, the sloping black and white profile of the Strata stands out. Much closer there is a great view of Rotherhithe – still a watery peninsula since its Surrey Docks days. Surviving jetties and quays between the new low-rise riverside residential estates give the regeneration a villagey look.

EAST

From the east window the Thames broadens out as it snakes downstream past the O_2 Arena on the tip of the Greenwich peninsula, with the Thames Barrier and the riverside Barrier Park beyond. Inland, the parallel waters of the former George V Dock – now City Airport – and Albert Dock illustrate how vast was the Victorians' achievement in building the old Royal Docks. In the far distance, 20 miles downstream, is the industrial-looking hub of Tilbury Docks – clearer at twilight as the lights appear.

The full curve of the Thames seen at dusk, with the sun setting behind the Shard. The horizon stretches all the way to Slough.

LLOYD'S OF LONDON

VIEWS ACROSS LONDON FROM A CITY 'CATHEDRAL'

In the year the Shard is due to open, Richard Rogers' Lloyd's Building turns 26 years old. In 1985 the sight of a stainless steel structure with blue cranes on the roof, open glass lifts, enclosed corner spiral staircases, jutting out toilet pods with portholes and external pipes and ducts climbing everywhere caused a sensation. Once a conservative City institution like Lloyd's insurance and reinsurance market had embraced the truly modern, however, the City's architectural floodgates opened to the variety of designs we see today. Internally, Lloyd's member syndicates have their offices in open booths on the first four floors around an indoor atrium with the double-height dealing floor at its base. Internal escalators serve these lower floors to keep market business moving efficiently. Above them the building is split into two on a vertical axis. The corporate floors, enclosed around the 'U' shape of the barrel-roofed atrium, rise up to the 11th floor.

Address One Lime Street, EC3M 7HA
Nearest Tube Bank

The windows in the common areas on the airy 11th floor of the Lloyd's Building, each overlooking a facet of the whole 360-degree view, chop up London into bite-sized skylines. In fact, the broadest accessible views (roughly 300 degrees) are from the two sets of enclosed glass lifts that hang off the building's west and north side elevations. Ascending and descending at smooth speed, they offer a fleeting but inviting flash of London, north, south and west.

SOUTH

Standing on the 11th floor looking across the three-sided empty atrium space from the base of its 'U', the seven-storey south-facing lancet window is like the east window behind the altar of a classical cathedral. This vast elongated rectangular slice of glass is cut into steel-framed sections all the way up to its fan shape at the top, some 213ft above ground. Two bold metal tubes brace the top two floors in an X-shaped cross. This brace and the window's external metal fretwork still allow a dramatic skyline view.

Through its panes the view is dominated not by green hills far away but by the concrete core of Raphael Viñoly's work-in-progress just a few

The twin towers of the Barbican flank the curved face of Moor House on London Wall with Drapers' Gardens in front.

yards away at 20 Fenchurch Street. Where 16th-century portraits of the Virgin and baby Jesus might present a background through an archway of the sun setting on a medieval village behind, we have instead from Lloyd's the curvaceous Strata with turbine silhouettes on the south London horizon. If this were a cathedral window, such a perspective would be inaccessible without an angel's wings.

Looking northeast through a window with a view restricted by the bulge of the Gherkin to the left and the smooth stainless steel curve of Lloyd's own emergency staircase to the right, the Olympic Stadium slips into full view. In the foreground stands the cruciform new office block of St Botolph's, banded in bright blue glass. This is architect Nicholas Grimshaw's recent contribution to the regeneration of the laggard Aldgate area.

NORTHWEST

Catch another slim view from a window largely obscured by enormous round air conditioning flues attached to the building's external façade. Tower 42 stands right outside, alongside the concrete core that will eventually be glazed to become the Pinnacle on Bishopsgate. The adjoining building site masked by tall hoardings at ground level belongs to Richard Rogers's new Leadenhall Building. This sliver of a view from the 11th floor reveals that the whole is just beginning to surface from its subterranean foundations.

Networks of giant cranes outnumber tall buildings in this small vista.

One, Poultry with St Paul's behind and the tower of the Royal Exchange in the foreground.

White Tower just behind and to the left. Here is one of those chance architectural period juxtapositions that might give the mistaken impression the City still favours Gothic architecture.

WEST

On the west side of the Lloyd's Building's 11th floor there are a couple of meeting rooms with broad span windows facing west. Through those, looking down Cornhill at the rear of the grand Royal Exchange that fronts onto Bank Junction, the detail shows that it is also a monument to its far-sighted originator, trader and one-time Lord Mayor Thomas Gresham. Dressed in Tudor breeches and bonnet, his stone statue stares out towards us from a niche in the tower that rises above the Exchange's 'back door' entrance. Above him his family emblem, the grasshopper, in gold on a gold spire tops the stone clock tower with lantern and cupola.

At Bank Junction itself, the flatiron edge of pinky-brown One, Poultry upstages the Lord Mayor's Mansion House before it. To the right, blue gantry cleaning cranes that jut out over the edge of Lloyd's roof above can't obscure a magnificent view of the 1920s Bank of England, rebuilt inside the fortress-like walls of John Soane's 1788 original.

Beyond those immediately below, Triton Court's tower rises up on the skyline at Finsbury Square with the figure of Mercury standing on a globe. Behind him, the half-finished concrete core of another tower sits on the horizon with a tall crane beside it. This one is all but abandoned; there is no target date for completion of the proposed affordable tower housing where City Road meets Old Street roundabout.

SOUTHEAST

From the southeast-facing side of Lloyd's, down one side of the walled-off glass atrium, on Eastcheap Minster Court's neo-Gothic pink and grey pointed granite towers with steeply gabled roofs frame the faux medieval towers of Tower Bridge and the genuine ones of the Tower of London's

SELFRIDGES ROOF GARDEN

A ONE-OFF WATERY VIEWPOINT FROM A LONDON RETAIL PALACE

In 1909 a thoroughly modern American millionaire from Wisconsin called Gordon Selfridge founded a revolution in retailing in London when he opened his department store on Oxford Street. His opening advertising campaign poster declared, 'no cards of admission are required . . . all are welcome'. In the same location for over a century through changes of ownership, depression, war and credit crunch, the name Selfridges remains synonymous with innovation, quality and high fashion retailing in the heart of the West End.

Address 400 Oxford Street, W1A 1AB
Nearest Tube Bond Street

Gordon Selfridge turned shopping into an experience, introducing department store features we take for granted today. It was his idea to design huge windows at street level featuring themed, well-lit window displays, thus creating the concept of window-shopping. Once attracted inside, shoppers could wander through a brightly lit, wide-aisled and high-ceilinged hall between islands of glass cases displaying the latest range of every kind of fashion article and accessory. The public had seen nothing like this before.

Selfridge understood there was a science behind successful retailing. The atmosphere must be relaxed to encourage browsing. A trained army of uniformed male and female sales assistants were present to offer help and advice – but only when approached. Beyond product purchasing from the start, Selfridges offered the public services like a news room, a post office, a travel and theatre ticket agency, library, bureau de change, ladies-only room, lunch hall and a range of novelty attractions like a rooftop soda fountain in summer.

Nine hydraulic lifts carrying shoppers between the six floors were another attraction. In the early years Selfridges' roof, mostly occupied by back-of-house utilities and two light wells for the store's upper floors – as it is today – offered temporary amusement activities such as an enclosed sub-target rifle range, a netted golf driving range, a venue for dances with live orchestra in the evenings and, one winter, an ice skating rink moved here from its

In 1928 the roof of Selfridges was a proper English country garden complete with croquet lawn.

original site at the Albert Hall.

In 1928 landscape architects took over 500 square feet of roof space and designed a series of permanent themed gardens leading into each other. Trellises and low walls surrounded a rock garden, a vine-covered walk and an English country garden complete with croquet lawn, ponds and dovecots. There were plenty of wooden garden seats too, where non-shoppers could linger.

The original high parapet wall that surrounded the entire roof was considered ample protection for customers up here. However newspapers reported at least three successful suicide attempts in the 1920s and 1930s. Photographs confirm the victims would have needed some kind of ladder to get onto the top of the wall – but jump off they did.

Between 1939 and 1945 Selfridges turned the gardens into a huge vegetable growing patch for the war effort. But the Blitz destroyed it all and the roof remained closed to the public until the summer of 2011,

when it reopened for a 'midsummer madness'-style campaign to promote a new low-calorie natural sweetener. The sponsors installed a steel-sided narrow boating lake complete with tiny rowing boats on water that was dyed emerald green. It took up most of the length of the parapet above Oxford Street. The whole installation was built onto a raised surface so that for the first time, from the boats, Selfridges' south-facing roof gardens could offer a skyline view.

From above one of Europe's noisiest and most crowded shopping streets, the calm and silent sea of Mayfair flats and hotel rooftops were exposed to rowers. Those red-brick residential blocks and five-storey houses around Duke Street, Grosvenor Square and most of Park Lane today would have housed the people who witnessed the arrival of Selfridges and the difference it made to London life. Apart from the construction of the new Park House right opposite and the Park Lane Hilton on the horizon, it is only the view from the rooftop that is broadly unchanged since the day Selfridges opened over 100 years ago.

THE BT TOWER

THE LONDON SKYLINE IN 20 MINUTES

The Ministry of Public Building and Works built the BT Tower, formerly known as the British Telecom Tower, the London Telecom Tower and originally the Post Office Tower, in 1965. By the 1960s London's growing need for transmission and reception of radios, televisions and telephones necessitated building a tower to hold VHF aerials. It immediately became a beloved cultural and architectural icon of London. Its famous revolving restaurant, Top of the Tower, run by Billy Butlin on the 34th floor, closed in 1980.

Address 60 Cleveland Street, W1T 4JZ
Nearest Tube Goodge Street

The tower structure is a 580ft tall cylinder supporting a 40ft weather radar aerial on top. Inevitably it sways in high winds but the addition of the wider viewing platforms towards the top helped stabilise its height. Today it is a Grade II listed building with a giant 360-degree LED display wrapped around its 36th and 37th floors to count down the days until the opening ceremony of the 2012 Olympic Games.

Permanently closed to the public except for the occasional charity or corporate event, the old restaurant took 20 minutes to complete a rotation – just long enough to enjoy the house speciality – Steak La Tour Ronde – while catching sight of London's earliest skyscrapers, Centre Point and the Hilton on Park Lane. The view from the restaurant is equally impressive today.

NORTH

Looking north but just below is the Fitzrovia area, named for Fitzroy Square – a circular island surrounded by trees. When Top of the Tower first opened, the Square provided access to the new Victoria Line, then under construction. Today its road is virtually shut off from the surrounding roads and is designated for pedestrians only.

Beyond Fitzrovia, there is a great view of Regent's Park. To the west side, where its tamed rose garden and theatre trail off towards the main boating lake, the white John Nash-designed terraces that line the park perimeter sport little white onion dome structures on their roofs as if they anticipated the 20th-century arrival of London's Central Mosque with its glinting golden dome and minaret tower, all visible from up here.

The Nash terraces march northwards in two parallel lines up the east side of the park, along Albany Street and the Outer Terrace as far as Camden Town and St John's Wood.

WEST

Looking due west, the parallel Devonshire, Weymouth and New Cavendish Streets – the widest east–west routes visible from here – cross the broader north–south avenue of Portland Place. Part of Marylebone's Portland Estate, altogether they form one of central London's unusual oases of grid-patterned streets. A patch of trees beyond indicates Paddington Street's Public Gardens and just behind

that, the double-roofed development called 55 Baker Street built on the former site of Marks & Spencer's headquarters stands out. Looking westward, there is only one tall white tower in view and that belongs to the University of Westminster.

The Portland Estate's northern boundary is marked by the sweeping semicircular row of off-white stucco terraces of Park Crescent at the northern tip of Great Portland Street. This, the southern entry point to the Regent's Park, completed Nash's 1811 processional route from Carlton House. Today Marylebone Road cuts it off from the park proper. On the far side of the main road, the park's southern edge is clearly defined by the houses of York Terrace and its rows of trees.

No longer the Top of the Tower revolving restaurant, but corporate events still afford a chance to take in the BT Tower's fabulous prospect of the capital.

This Sixties visitor thought the view from the Post Office Tower was the greatest.

EAST

Ahead of us is the side of Bloomsbury close to the Euston Road. The view reveals clearly the layout of William Wilkins's classical 1829 University College campus on Gower Street with its fine white Doric columned entrance on the far side of the quadrangle. On the opposite side of Gower Street to Wilkins's building there is a rare view from above of the complex cruciform structure of Alfred Waterhouse's University College Hospital. Built about 75 years later, it could barely be more 'opposite' in style. Invisible from street level, its four giant crimson brick wings with steep gabled grey slate roofs are each crossed by another shorter wing. Where the end of each main wing meets the street, its corner is emphasised with an ornate turret and spire.

Clumps of trees tucked between layers of university faculty buildings indicate the locations of Bloomsbury's character-forming squares. Between them successive architects over the last 150 years have shoehorned buildings into the tight spaces. Only the broad sweep of Denys Lasdun's Institute of Education down the length of Bedford Way was given enough space to compete with Charles Holden's monumental Senate House, built 43 years earlier. His stripped-down version of a classical building with an elaborate tower dominates the foreground view. Behind lies a pleasant vignette of the City of London, with Canary Wharf beyond.

TRELLICK TOWER

ONE OF LONDON'S MOST POLITICALLY CHARGED URBAN SKYLINES

Trellick Tower was the late architect Erno Goldfinger's interpretation of Bauhaus chic for London. A 1960s residential skyscraper, it was the tallest in London at the time its 31 storeys were commissioned by the Royal Borough of Kensington and Chelsea. Its controversial impact on the local landscape has never ceased. Day and night it catches the motorist's eye along Westway – the equally controversial high-level motorway built through west London at the same period. Architectural reappraisal resulted in Trellick Tower's Grade II listing and subsequent rehabilitation. An increasing number of private owners have since bought flats from a desire to live within its 'historic' roughened-up concrete walls. Externally it is a building in two parts, making it uniquely identifiable on the skyline; its services and utilities are housed in a skinny separate tower, linked on every third floor by a covered walkway to the Tower proper.

Address Near Golborne Road, W10 5PS
Nearest Tube Westbourne Park

Trellick Tower's 1966 design pre-dated that of Westway, although it was not completed until two years after the urban motorway opened. Looking south from the 30th floor, it is as if it was purpose-built to witness how, by building this raised road, urban planners succeeded in destroying long-established residential communities to leave a swathe of wasteland below. If anyone could ever doubt London's resilience and powers of survival in the face of adversity, this view would be testimony par excellence. It must be one of London's most politically charged urban skylines.

Looking immediately below, it is obvious that this neighbourhood had to contend with more than its share of public amenities for years before Westway arrived. First, the Grand Union Canal encircled the area, cutting through dense urban tracts into Paddington Basin. Then the Great Western Railway bisected swathes of surrounding streets. Finally, both the Hammersmith and City and Circle tube lines rose above ground here, passing the fronts and backs of homes. By 1970 locals knew the final coup, in the form of Westway, was about to be delivered to west London neighbourhoods north of Bayswater and Notting Hill.

The urban motorway rendered hundreds of 19th-century terraced homes uninhabitable, their upstairs

The dense corrugation of northwest London, from the top of the Trellick Tower..

rooms just a few metres from its concrete sides. Since then the local council and the Kensington Housing Trust have tried to compensate local residents with better quality low-rise estates in brick, like the one around St Ervan's Road just below the Trellick Tower. Following much of the old street pattern, although still partially cordoned off by Westway and the tube lines, overall its human height and scale fits snugly into the existing leafy, pedestrian-friendly streets.

SOUTHWEST

Broadly speaking, from the Trellick's top-floor southwest-facing window the view divides into a 'before and after Westway' picture. 'Before' are the surviving streets with pretty, part pastel-stuccoed four-storey terraces – some with ground floor shops and corner pubs. These characterise London west of Paddington as it was built up from the mid 19th century. 'After' is a curious infill-patterned landscape where some old but mostly new housing has been kettled into triangular and crescent-shaped dead ends by the curves of the tube lines and Westway by Westbourne Park Station. The Trellick Tower itself is

Trelllick Tower's historic roughened-concrete walls are now listed.

part of the Trellick and Edenham Estate on Elkstone Road. Across the railway, about a quarter of a mile away, is the Wornington Green Estate and Athlone Gardens where Wornington Road meets the top of Portobello Road. The long-term effect of such developments has been to shield most of the immediate area from the gentrification that began decades ago in neighbouring Ladbroke Grove and Portobello Road.

From up here there are signs that the vibe is visibly changing. A big empty brown earth site slightly to the northwest indicates that some of the older council estates are coming down, although actual building

appears to have stalled. Almost directly below Trellick Tower, some of the Portuguese and Moroccan grocers and cafes geared to and run by the older generation of post-Second World War immigrants in the pretty Golborne Road, a shopping street determinedly holding together the residential community, are being supplanted by high-fashion celebrity names.

NORTHEAST

From the window on the opposite side, Hampstead Heath and Highgate Hill frame the horizon. The urban landscape between the Tower and the foothills appears compressed

The languid passage of the Grand Union Canal and the hectic traffic of the Westway intermingle in this northeastern view.

and these two high spots look much closer than they are. The Grand Union Canal meanders immediately below the tower on this side. New and old residential terraces line both sides and behind those on the far side, the Harrow Road becomes traceable.

Just beyond this peaceful foreground, suddenly the urban pattern dramatically changes. Row upon row of terraced house roofs are lined up together in a huge but tightly packed quarter. This is low-rise Kensal Town and West Kilburn, built at the turn of the 20th century. At street level it feels comfortably normal but from up above this is late Victorian high-density urban housing. It separates itself from the urban landscape of Queen's Park and Willesden Cemetery just beyond like a town within a town. To the west the streets become broad and more salubrious in appearance, with the older part-stucco terraced houses and tall brick mansion flats of Maida Vale. In lieu of parks, those residents have Paddington Recreation Ground, its football pitches and goal posts visible from up here.